Facing the Future

A Guide for Parents of Young People
Who Have Sexually Abused

Simon Hackett

Russell House Publishing

First published in 2001 by:
Russell House Publishing Ltd.
4 St. George's House
Uplyme Road
Lyme Regis
Dorset DT7 3LS

Tel: 01297-443948
Fax: 01297-442722
e-mail: help@russellhouse.co.uk

British Library Cataloguing-in-publication Data:
A catalogue record for this book is available from the British Library.

ISBN: 1-898924-94-5

Typeset by The Hallamshire Press Limited, Sheffield.
Printed by Bell and Bain, Glasgow

Although the case examples are real, the names have been changed to
protect the anonymity of the people involved.

About Russell House Publishing

RHP is a group of social work, probation, education and youth and community work
practitioners and academics working in collaboration with a professional publishing
team. Our aim is to work closely with the field to produce innovative and valuable
materials to help managers, trainers, practitioners and students.
We are keen to receive feedback on publications and new ideas for future projects.

Contents

List of Exercises for Parents

Acknowledgements

This book owes much to the parents and children who have so courageously shared their stories and experiences with me about the sexual abuse that has affected their lives. Although I am not able to name individuals, I am thankful particularly to the parents with whom I have worked in the Kaleidoscope parents' group in Sunderland and at G-MAP in Manchester. I have been lucky to share many of the experiences reflected in the book with valued colleagues at both of these projects. Dave O'Callaghan and Bobbie Print from G-MAP have been pioneers in this work, allies and friends for ten years and their untiring commitment to young people who have abused remains an inspiration. Paula Telford has shown me the kindness and support that has meant that I can contribute to the work of Kaleidoscope whilst at the same time combining this with the demands of research and teaching at the University of Durham. My thanks also go to Martin Calder who has supported this project enthusiastically since its inception.

About the author

Simon Hackett is a Lecturer at the University of Durham in the Centre for Applied Social Studies. A qualified social worker, Simon was previously Programme Director of G-MAP, an organisation based in Manchester which he helped to set up and which works with children and young people who sexually abuse. In total, he has over ten years of experience in this field of work and is a consultant to a number of programmes across the country. He continues to work with children and young people with sexually harmful behaviours at Kaleidoscope in Sunderland, where he has also been part of a groupwork programme for parents.

Introduction

Initial Considerations

I have written this book because I wanted to help parents come to terms with what are often the devastating consequences of finding out that a child they have parented has sexually abused another person, or has behaved in a sexually inappropriate way. If your child has hurt someone as a result of his sexually abusive or problematic behaviour, then this book is for you.

Throughout ten years of work with children with sexual behaviour problems and their families I have been impressed by the courage shown by so many of the children and their parents, whose support and willingness to contribute to the work has so often made the difference between the success and failure of attempts by professionals to help. I feel that I have been privileged to have been able to do this work and I have learnt a great deal from the children, young people and parents who have shared with me their difficulties and problems.

A book like this can never be an adequate replacement for the support of a trained and understanding professional person, who will be able to add her experience to the points included here. One of the most important messages from the book is that dealing with sexually abusive or problematic behaviour by your child is one of the most isolating experiences that can happen to you as a parent. The consequences of your child's behaviour can affect all parts of your life; your feelings about yourself and others, your relationships, your innermost thoughts and the way in which you go about your day-to-day life. Breaking this isolation by gaining the support of a trusted professional, someone who is not going to reject you or hurt you, is one important stride you can make towards helping your child come to terms with his behaviour. However difficult it is now, it is important to keep hold of the fact that things can change and move forward. As suggested in the title of this book, you **can** have a 'future' following your child's abuse and your child **can** lead a life which is free from abuse.

> At the beginning I thought I had lost everything, my son, my whole life came tumbling down around me. Now I know that I have lost some things, but there are many more things that I have found as a result that I didn't have before…if this had not happened, I wouldn't be this strong now.
>
> (Mother of a 14 year old boy who abused his brother)

I have structured the book into sections, each of which raises important themes. I have decided upon these themes after listening to parents, whose children have abused, talk about their own experiences and raise questions which were important for them. The book contains examples of the words, feelings and experiences of a range of parents. You may find that some of them are similar to how you feel, others may not apply to you. There is no single way that a parent has to feel or react, nor are there likely to be simple answers to the difficult questions that sexual abuse by your child raises.

A book of this kind cannot possibly hope to offer you all that you need, nor can it take away from the painful struggles that you may be going through now. However, I hope that you will find something in *Facing the Future* to draw strength from, or something that will help you and your family with a particular problem that you have.

How to use this Book

Cover to cover?

This book can be used in a number of ways. Some parents will want to read the book through from start to finish, others may feel that it is necessary to go straight to a section which is of particular concern to them. The process of coming to terms with these issues can be like a difficult journey. Things may seem very different at the end of the journey compared with the beginning. I hope that you can use the book as a source of information and that you will find it to be valuable, no matter where you are on this journey at the moment.

The seven chapters in the book follow a pattern which take you from understanding some of the basic issues, to finding out about the abuse, helping your child and your family, to considering the future. At various points in the text there are 'summary points' which contain key messages from the section which has gone before and 'questions to ask yourself' which are an attempt to encourage you to think about the relevance of the points being made to your own situation. The chapters are meant to build upon each other and there are benefits in tackling them in the order that they are presented. However, the path to recovery following abuse is rarely simple and straightforward and, as you work on these difficult issues, you may need to go back and forward in the book a number of times. Some sections of the book are likely to be more relevant to your own situation than others and my advice would be to pick out those which are particularly important for you and to spend more time on these if necessary.

How to use the exercises in the book

I also offer a range of exercises for parents to complete which are linked to the material in each chapter. The exercises come at the end of the appropriate section in each chapter. There is, of course, a limit to how useful a written exercise can be, but completing the exercises can help you to focus on, and make sense of, your own situation. The exercises need time and careful consideration. You may wish to share the work you do on the exercises with a partner or supporter. Doing this may help the different people involved to share their feelings and perspectives in a way which does not 'just happen' in normal conversation.

With or without professional support?

It may be that this book has been given to you by a professional who is offering a service to your family. If this is the case, it will probably be helpful for you to talk with the professional about how best you can use the material in the book to support the work with you and your child. You may wish to share your thoughts, responses and the completed exercises with the professional in order to gain her views.

Other parents may well have bought this book directly, or may have had only a brief involvement from a professional. If so, I would recommend strongly that you think very carefully about gaining some support in coping with the difficult issues that may be raised in tackling abusive behaviour from your child and in reading this book. This person does not necessarily need to be a professional, and you may not need to go into detail about the issues you are facing, but having someone who knows that you may be feeling down or struggling with difficult feelings is essential. Many parents are highly anxious that friends, neighbours and family members should not find out about the abuse and, as a result, are forced to live a very isolated life after the abuse has come to light. Choosing the right kind of supporter, someone who is not going to use the information against you and who will keep an open mind, is therefore an important consideration. If there is no-one you know who can offer you this, then you could use one of the anonymous telephone counselling and advice services that offer parents support. A list is included at the back of this book. If you live in a relationship with another person, particularly if you share the parenting of a child with sexually abusive or problematic behaviour, I would advise you to talk through these issues with your partner. In my experience, a child's abusive behaviour can expose cracks and stresses in relationships, but the need to come together to help your child can also bring relationships closer. It is important that your child is given consistent messages from both parents and that one person is not perceived by your child as taking the problem less seriously than the other.

A health warning

Although it may seem an obvious point, it is necessary to offer a 'health warning' at this point at the beginning of the book. In dealing with the subject of young people's sexual behaviours, the book contains explicit sexual content and talks very frankly about the kinds of sexual behaviours displayed by children and young people. The need to connect children, sex and abuse in this way is something that the majority of parents, thankfully, do not need to do. However, finding out that your child has abused or has a sexual behaviour problem forces you to do this. If you find yourself upset or emotionally affected in other ways by any aspect of the book, it may be helpful to talk this through with a partner, professional or supporter. How to deal with the feelings you might have after you find out about your child's behaviours and how to cope in the longer-term is discussed in Chapters 2 and 4 respectively.

Do I need to be a birth parent to use this book?

I use the word 'parent' in the book to describe someone who has, or who has had, caring responsibilities for a child who has sexually abused. Although I write about particular issues that can affect long-term carers and families, you do not have to be a 'natural' or birth parent to benefit from this book. It may well be that step-parents, adoptive parents or foster carers will be able to use the book to deal with their own situations.

Does my child need to be living with me in order for me to be able to use this book?

Many young people who have sexually abused or shown inappropriate sexual behaviours carry on living at home as before. However, some young people are required to move away from home once abuse has been discovered. This is particularly the case when the victim is living in the same house, if there are other vulnerable or younger children in the house or if the young person who has abused is seen as being at risk in some way at home. Sometimes when young people are asked to move after abusing, they live with relatives such as grandparents. Other young people may go into in a foster home or a children's home. Whether your child is living with you now, and however likely or unlikely it is your child will return to your home in the future, it is important that you have support, that you learn about why the abuse may have taken place and that you think about how you can help your child make the changes needed for a future without abuse. So, this book is for you regardless of where your child is living at the present time and regardless of whether your child will come back to live with you.

Why does the book distinguish between children and young people?

One of the dilemmas in writing a book for parents of children who have sexually abused is whether to try to focus upon all ages from birth to eighteen or whether to select out a particular age range. Professionals who work in this field have become more aware over the years of the differences between younger children who have sexually problematic behaviours and a teenager who sexually abuses. For example, it is clearly not fair or appropriate to approach the following two children in the same way:

- A four-year-old boy who has been abused himself and who is reacting to this experience by acting out his own abuse in 'sex games' with other children.
- A fifteen-year-old who sexually assaults a five-year-old with physical threats and force.

Because of the very big differences in younger children and teenagers, I have focused most of the attention of this book on 'young people' by which I mean children in the ten to eighteen years age range. Much of the content and many of the exercises may be appropriate for parents of children who fall outside of this age range, but there are some important reasons for focusing on this age range. Firstly, this is a peak age of sexually problematic behaviours and one when physical changes to the body are taking place and where the whole issue of sex is assuming great importance to young people. Secondly, the age of criminal responsibility in the UK is ten years old and the system for dealing with children under ten is therefore different from dealing with those who can be seen in law as 'criminally responsible' for their actions. If you wish to look at material which focuses specifically on much younger children with sexual behaviour problems, there are some suggested resources included at the end of this book.

Boys or girls?

The problem of writing about young people's sexually abusive behaviour in a way which is sensitive to issues of gender but makes the book relevant for parents of both young men and young women who abuse has been a dilemma for me. You will find that I refer to the 'young person and *his* needs' and 'the victim and *her* needs' throughout this book. This is not to suggest that all young people who abuse are male and all victims are female, but is done to simplify the language and to help distinguish between the abuser and the victim. You should bear in mind that both the young person who has abused and the victim can be of either sex. I am not trying to suggest that there are equal numbers of boys and girls who abuse, but merely that parents need help to deal with the consequences of sexually abusive behaviour regardless of whether their child is male or female.

Indeed we know that the vast majority of those who show sexually abusive behaviour are males. This is true in young people as it is in adults. However, there is growing awareness and recognition that a small percentage of people who sexually abuse are females, including in the adolescent age range. Studies suggest that between 2% and 7% of young people who sexually abuse may be female (Calder, 2001). As yet, we do not know enough about the differences and similarities between young men and young women who sexually abuse. However, from my experience of working with a small number of parents of young women who have sexually abused, I know that many of the issues they face and many of their worries and concerns are similar to those of parents of young men. Although they may be a minority, I do not wish to exclude parents of girls from the help that the book can provide.

Guidance for professionals on using the book

If you are a professional working with parents whose children have abused, you may wish to use this Guide as a sourcebook for enhancing your practice with parents. You may wish to give the book in its entirety to parents or you may prefer to select sections and resources that are applicable to a particular situation. However you choose to use this resource, I have found it important to allow time to parents who may be in a very real crisis situation to work through the complex issues raised. Questions can emerge for parents at any time of the day and having a source of written information and guidance can help with the many times when questions arise away from family sessions.

This book seeks to provide parents with both a source of practical information and emotional support, as well as the opportunity, through a range of therapeutic exercises, to think in depth about their own situations. Given the overwhelming emotions that so often are promoted for parents following the discovery of the abuse, we should not expect parents to be able to digest lots of information clearly, especially at the beginning of professional intervention. I have found that many parents need to return time and again to core questions as their understandings grow over the months following the discovery of the abuse. It is my hope that a written resource of support and information, as attempted in this book, will be helpful in this process.

Facing the Future as a Process

The shape of this book reflects a number of stages that parents may need to address in order to be able to face the future following their child's sexually abusive behaviour. This process will not be the same for everyone, but it is important to ensure that you have adequately addressed each of the steps in your own way. The process can be represented as follows and each step is covered in a later chapter in the book, as indicated:

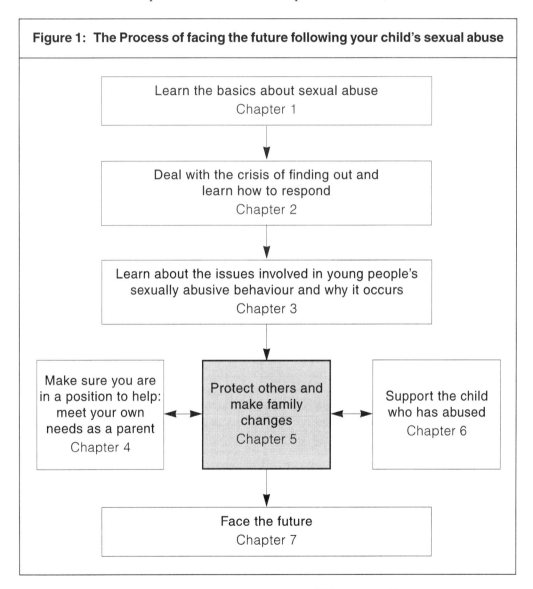

Figure 1: The Process of facing the future following your child's sexual abuse

Learn the basics about sexual abuse
Chapter 1

Deal with the crisis of finding out and learn how to respond
Chapter 2

Learn about the issues involved in young people's sexually abusive behaviour and why it occurs
Chapter 3

Make sure you are in a position to help: meet your own needs as a parent
Chapter 4

Protect others and make family changes
Chapter 5

Support the child who has abused
Chapter 6

Face the future
Chapter 7

Learn the basics about sexual abuse (Chapter 1)

First of all, it is important to open your mind to the issues that you are going to have to face. This involves understanding what young people's sexual abuse is and how it differs from normal childhood sexual experimentation. It also includes understanding the meaning of the various terms that you are likely to hear. In particular, you should consider what you know about your child's sexual behaviour and why you and others should be concerned.

xii Facing the Future

Deal with the crisis of finding out and learn how to respond (Chapter 2)

Parents often feel that their lives have been turned upside down as a result of the abuse. You need to be able to deal with your immediate crisis situation. This involves thinking about what to do after you have found out about the abuse and looking at how to respond to your child, as well as how to deal with denial, your feelings and issues of blame and responsibility.

Learn about the issues involved in young people's sexually abusive behaviour and why it occurs (Chapter 3)

It is important to make sure you have all the necessary information about what is known about children and young people's sexually abusive behaviour, so that you can make sense of why this has happened to your child and in your family. This knowledge will help you challenge any myths surrounding the issues and will be the foundation upon which you can rebuild your life.

Make sure you are in a position to help: meet your own needs as a parent (Chapter 4)

Discovering that your child has sexually abused can leave you with difficult long-term feelings and emotions. You need to be stable enough and coping well enough in order to make sure you are doing all you possibly can to help your child and to protect other children. This may involve reviewing your parenting style and developing new parenting skills.

Protect others and make family changes (Chapter 5)

This contains perhaps the most important aspect of what you can do as a parent. In reality you need to be doing this all the way through the process, which is why this stage is emphasised in the diagram above. It means ensuring that others in your family who may be vulnerable are protected, knowing what you can do to monitor or watch for worrying incidents and whether, when and how you should trust your child again. Making it safe for yourself, your family, the victims of the abuse, the child who has abused and the community is the backbone of facing the future.

Support the child who has sexually abused (Chapter 6)

This involves understanding the professional and legal system and the responsibilities this places upon you as a parent. It is also about how you can work with professionals; what you can expect from them and what you can do as a parent to help your child face up to their abusive behaviours. It means contributing to any work done by professionals, but also knowing how you can talk to your child about the abuse and how you can encourage your child to develop a healthy sexual identity.

Face the future (Chapter 7)

This final step is about facing the future and finding hope. This is about learning to live once the professionals have gone, understanding what the abuse will mean for the future and how to cope and respond in the years ahead. If your family has been split following the abuse, it is also about when and in what circumstances you should consider bringing the young person who has abused back into your family home.

Chapter 1
Understanding the Issues

An Introduction to Important Terminology

Terms you may hear from professionals

I have tried to write this book in a way which is clear and understandable to parents who may never before have had reason to think about, or read about, sexual abuse. It may be that your family has had no previous contact with professionals such as social workers, psychologists or police officers. Even if you are used to having professionals involved in your life, you may not be familiar with the terms that are used to describe your child's sexual behaviour, nor the work being done to try to stop the abuse.

There is a huge amount of different terminology used by professionals to describe the kind of problems associated with sexually abusive behaviour of a child or young person. Sometimes terms are confusing and do not say a great deal to people who are not specialists in the field. Here are some of the common key terms you may hear, with a brief definition:

- **Sexual abuse** is the term which is most widely used to describe sexual behaviour which is *unacceptable, harmful* and *wrong*. When applied to children and young people, this does **not** include sexual behaviours that are a normal part of children's development, but it is used to say that there was some kind of force or pressure involved or that somehow one of the people involved was 'victimised' by the other. These issues are considered in more detail later in this chapter.

- **Sexual aggression** is a term used similarly to sexual abuse to describe sexual behaviours that are wrong and harmful. Adolescents might be referred to as being 'sexually aggressive' if they have sexually abused another person, especially if they have used physical force. The use of the word 'aggression' reminds us that sexually abusive behaviours committed by young people may include force, trickery or violence.

- **Sexually inappropriate behaviour** is a term sometimes used by professionals instead of 'sexually abusive behaviour' to describe sexual behaviour by children and young people that is a problem. It sometimes describes sexual behaviours that appear to be in part consenting, but that are nevertheless regarded as wrong for the child's age and development. With sexually problematic behaviours, it may be that neither of the children involved was made into a victim or was harmed or hurt during the sexual behaviours, but the behaviours still need to stop. This term is also frequently used to refer to younger children's sexual behaviours.

- **Sexually reactive** is a term which professionals use in order to describe younger children (usually under ten years of age) who may be 'reacting to' or acting out sexually abusive behaviour that they have experienced. This term is commonly used for younger children whom, because they are so close to their own experiences of being sexually abused, it is not appropriate to describe as 'abusers'. Very young children who are sexually reactive may be unaware that their behaviour is wrong and are copying and repeating behaviours that they have experienced. You may also hear the term **abuse reactive** which means the same as sexually reactive.

- **Sexual offence** is a term to describe a sexual act that is against the law. Strictly speaking, a **sexual offender** is someone who has been cautioned or convicted of a sexual offence and the terms **adolescent sexual offender** or **juvenile sexual offender** are commonly used to describe young people who have been convicted of such an offence.

- **Paedophile** is a term that most parents will be familiar with through the media. It is commonly used to describe any person who has committed a sexual offence, although it really refers to adult sexual offenders who have a sexual preference for children. The diagnosis of a paedophile is a matter for a psychiatrist and requires the person to be 16 years old. So, this is a term that should not be used to describe children or young people under 16.

- **Perpetrator** is used to describe someone who has committed (or 'perpetrated') an offence, in this case a sexually abusive act. Calling young people 'perpetrators' or 'abusers' or 'offenders' is problematic as this leaves out the 'child' or 'young person' and suggests that they are merely being seen in terms of what they have done.

- **Schedule One Offender** refers to someone who has been convicted of an offence of violence against children under the age of 18. The particular offences are listed in Schedule One of the Children and Young Persons Act 1933 and may be violent physical or sexual offences. A person convicted of one of these offences is commonly referred to as a 'Schedule One Offender'. If a person has a Schedule One conviction, the authorities (social services, probation and police) are required to make an assessment of the risk that the person might pose to other people in the home or in the community.

- **Victim** is an important term which describes the other person involved in the sexually abusive act. The use of the word victim indicates that this person was forced, tricked or coerced into the behaviours, that they could not say no, or that they did not understand the consequences of saying yes. Adults who were sexually abused as children are often known as **survivors** of abuse to distinguish them from child victims and to recognise their strength in having lived with, and coped with, the consequences of their childhood abuse.

- **Sibling sexual abuse** refers to sexual abuse where one sibling (brother or sister) has abused another. See Chapter 2 for more details.

- **Assessment** means a professional (or group of professionals working together) finding out about a child's situation and his behaviours, making a judgement on what may have contributed to the development of the behaviours and trying to work out how best to help. Professionals may talk about a 'comprehensive' or 'core' assessment to describe this. A **risk assessment** is part of an overall assessment which attempts to work out what risks a young person may present to other people and what can be done to minimise the likelihood that the young person will sexually abuse again. An assessment is required before any structured 'treatment' work can be done, to make sure that this work will give the young person the best opportunity to stop abusing.

- **Treatment** is a common name given to describe the work done with children and young people to help them to stop the abusive behaviours. Other terms that you may hear are **intervention**, **therapy** or **therapeutic work**. All of these terms may refer to individual work with your child. If your child is offered treatment or therapy together with other young people, this is referred to as **group treatment** or **groupwork**. Sometimes professionals will talk about **cognitive behavioural work** which refers to the particular theoretical approach that is most commonly used in work to help young people who have abused. Other terms you may hear in relation to work done with your child include **relapse prevention work** (a technical term which means trying to prevent the abuse from starting again) and **victim empathy work** (which means getting a young person to think about the impact of their actions upon their victim). Chapter 6 goes into detail about such work, how you can contribute and how you can support your child in it.

- **Registers:** There are two different registers that you may hear about. One is the **Child Protection Register** which is kept in each local area by social services on behalf of all the professional agencies to make a record of children who might need protection because they are at risk of some kind of abuse or harm. Children who have sexually abused may be placed on the child protection register because they are at risk in some way, or more commonly, their siblings may be registered. **The Sex Offender Register** is a different list of people (both adults and young people) who have a conviction or a caution for a sexual offence. This is held by the police and there is a responsibility for all those on this register (and parents in the case of young people) to inform the police where they are living and whenever they change address. Chapter 6 describes the professional system in more detail, including what it might require of you as parents.

If in any doubt about any of these terms, or other terms or words that a professional uses, ask. Remember that most people have not had to learn about sexual abuse and have never needed to think about these technical terms or professional language before. It may also be that you object or disagree with the implications of a professional using a certain word or term, as you think it unfairly represents your child or your family. In such cases, it is important that you talk this through with the other person to see why she is using this term and to discuss why this makes you uncomfortable or unsure. This should be seen as a sign that you are a concerned parent who wishes to take the problem seriously.

Terms used in this book

Throughout the book, I use the term **young people who have sexually abused** to refer to children of ten to eighteen years old who have shown unacceptable and harmful sexual behaviours. This age range is quite wide however. For example a ten-year-old and a seventeen-year-old are generally at very different stages of their development and have different social and sexual needs. It is therefore important to see your child as an individual with his own needs. At certain points in the book I also talk about 'younger children' by which I am referring to children up to the age of ten.

I recognise that the term 'young person who has sexually abused' is quite clumsy and long, but I avoid using the shorter 'young abuser' or 'adolescent offender' as, for me, these terms describe the child only by what he has done wrong. It is important not to downplay what a young person has done or make it seem less serious by using language which does not fit with the abuse. However, we should always consider the messages that might be communicated beneath the words we use. Consider the following statements, for example:

The terms:	The messages that might be communicated to a young person by the words:
'You are a sexual abuser'	• All you are is an abuser • You are still an abuser • You will always be an abuser • I am only interested in you as an abuser
'You are a young person who has sexually abused'	• You are a young person first and foremost • You have done something wrong but this doesn't mean to say that you will always be an abuser • You could change • I am taking your behaviour seriously: it is abuse, but I am interested in you as a young person as well

At places in the book, it has been necessary for me to make a distinction between **sexually abusive behaviours** and **sexually inappropriate behaviours**. The dividing line between behaviours that should be considered as 'abusive' and what is only 'inappropriate' is sometimes difficult to draw, but the basic distinction is that sexually inappropriate behaviour may not necessarily involve a victim. For instance consider the two following examples:

- Jamie is 14. His girlfriend Amy is 12. Jamie asks Amy to have full sex with him. He doesn't put any pressure on Amy. Amy is not altogether sure about this because of their age, but they talk this through and agree to try it out. Afterwards, they are worried that Amy might be pregnant and that someone might find out what they have done.
- Alan is 14. His girlfriend Jane is 12. Alan asks Jane to have full sex. She says no, but Alan won't take 'no' for an answer and puts more and more pressure on Jane, who is still not sure. In the end, Alan pins Jane down and forces her to have sex with him.

Thinking about these two situations as the parents of the children, or the professionals involved with them, we might agree that both situations are not appropriate for the children concerned and should stop or be changed. In both situations we might feel that having full sexual intercourse is not appropriate and is illegal at this age and that there are health risks for the young people. But we would probably agree that the second example is much more serious and that Alan has abused Jane. The first one is inappropriate and illegal and the behaviours might have unhelpful consequences, but we might conclude that there is no individual who is being victimised here. It would be unfair to label either Jamie or Amy as an 'abuser' in this case, although we could perhaps talk about them engaging in inappropriate sexual behaviours.

Finding the right words to describe your situation

Remember that your child is a young person first and foremost. Your child is not defined by his sexually problematic behaviours or the offence he has committed. However, you should think carefully about the words that you can use to describe what has happened. For instance, it would be wrong and unfair to use the term paedophile to describe a young girl of seven who was repeating in her own behaviour some of the ways in which she was sexually abused. At the same time, to talk about 'sexually inappropriate behaviour' in relation to a seventeen-year-old young man who has committed a violent rape would be disrespectful to the victim concerned.

It is important then for you as parents to find the correct language for the abuse that your child has committed: language which shows your child, and professionals who may be involved, that you understand the seriousness of the behaviours and their consequences. Language that is either *unfairly harsh* to your child or *unfairly disrespectful* to the victim should be avoided. Sometimes, finding the right language can be difficult and you may need to review this over time as you develop more knowledge of what happened. It can be helpful to check with a partner, supporter or professional to gain advice on the words you are using. However, if you avoid saying in plain language to your child that you consider the behaviour to be abuse, he might feel that you are unconcerned.

Summary points from this section

- Sexual abuse is a difficult subject to talk about, but it is important to find the right kinds of words to be able to communicate with your child, other people in your family and professionals.
- The language you use should match the seriousness of what has happened and let people know how you view the behaviours.
- The words should reflect that your child is a child first and that the sexual behaviours are behaviours not the whole person.
- Checking out language and talking terms through with your partner, supporter or a professional involved with your child can help.

Questions to consider

- Are you using terms that suggest the behaviours were either more or less serious than they were?
- Are there other terms that would be more suitable for you to use?
- Are you able to distinguish between your child's sexually abusive behaviour and other more positive aspects of your child?

Exercise 1: Thinking about words to describe your situation

Purpose. This exercise provides you with an opportunity to consider the best words for your own situation.

1. Think about the following words. Put a ring around any that help to describe the situation with your child. Use the space underneath the words to write down why you have chosen the words you have ringed.

Exposure   Violent   Unfair   Hurt

Aggressive   Sexual abuse   Rape

Assault   Experimenting   Victim   Harmful

Denial   Cruel   Lying

Mistake   Offence

Not serious   Serious

2. I have chosen these words because:

....

....

....

3. Other words I need to add are:

....

....

....

Understanding Sexual Abuse

What is sexually abusive behaviour?

One of the important things to consider in the early stages of finding out that your child has behaved in a sexually abusive or inappropriate way is what other people are worried about, even if you do not necessarily share all of their concerns. For some parents, it will be very clear from what you have heard or seen that your child's behaviour is 'abuse'. For other parents, it can be hard to understand what has happened, why it is causing other people concern, or why the word 'abuse' is being used at all. Being clear about what sexual abuse is and why your child's behaviour is a problem is an important first step following the discovery of the behaviours.

Defining normal, problematic or abusive sexual behaviours has been a difficulty for professionals. On some occasions there are grey areas and it is not clear whether a young person's behaviour fits into one category or another. The uncertainty created can make us feel powerless to respond to behaviours that trouble or concern us. Many parents too have talked about feeling very confused about what is and is not normal in children's sexual behaviours and have said that the discovery of their child's abusive behaviour has made them unsure about their own sexual knowledge and experiences.

Thinking about children's sexual behaviours on a continuum

One helpful way of thinking about a child's sexually problematic and abusive behaviours is to imagine a continuum of sexual behaviours. On the one extreme of the continuum are the kinds of sexual behaviours that are common and generally seen by most people as acceptable. On the other extreme are behaviours that are obviously wrong and harmful. In the middle is the 'grey area' where the behaviours might be more normal or not normal depending on other things. The idea of this 'continuum' can be represented as follows:

Figure 2: A continuum of sexual behaviours

Clearly OK	Somewhere in the middle: the grey area	Clearly not OK: abusive
←		→
Normal for the age of the child	Not sure: could be normal or not normal, depending on certain things…	Not normal for the age of the child

The idea of a continuum helps to show that there are some sexual behaviours that parents and professionals should be more worried about than others. It also shows us that sometimes simply knowing about the behaviour itself is often not enough to be able to make a decision as to whether it was OK or not. Here are the two examples from earlier in this chapter which involved children of the same ages in the same sexual activity:

- Jamie is 14. His girlfriend Amy is 12. Jamie asks Amy to have full sex with him. He doesn't put any pressure on Amy. Amy is not altogether sure about this because of their age, but they talk this through and agree to try it out. Afterwards, they are worried that Amy might be pregnant and that someone might find out what they have done.

- Alan is 14. His girlfriend Jane is 12. Alan asks Jane to have full sex. She says no, but Alan won't take 'no' for an answer and puts more and more pressure on Jane, who is still not sure. In the end, Alan pins Jane down and forces her to have sex with him.

Where on the continuum would you put Alan's behaviour and where would you put Jamie's behaviour? What ideas are helpful for you in making a decision about where to place the behaviours? Share your thoughts on this with your partner or supporter, if you have one.

Looking at for whom and why the sexual behaviour is a problem

Clearly, trying to place your child's behaviour on a continuum of the kinds of behaviours we might expect and accept from children and young people is not enough in itself to understand why it is not acceptable or why we should be concerned. Behaviours that might be OK in one situation or 'context' may be totally unacceptable in others, as you saw in the two examples above.

So, one helpful way of thinking about problematic or abusive behaviour is to consider *who the behaviour is a problem for* and *why it is a problem* (O'Callaghan and Print, 1994). Figure 3 is designed to show how we can 'weigh up' a child's sexual behaviour as problematic or abusive according to a number of factors.

Thinking about consent and power

Two important ideas that can help us to think about what is and what is not abusive in children's sexual behaviour are **consent** and **power** (O'Callaghan and Print, 1994).

Consent is about the ability of a person to agree to a sexual act. The basic idea is that any sexual behaviour in which the people involved do not fully 'consent' or agree can be seen as abusive. Although this is quite a straightforward definition, the issue of consent is far from simple to establish in cases involving children and young people. For example, some young people try to suggest that the child they abused was a willing participant who agreed to the sexual behaviours. Simply saying 'yes' to something that is suggested may, on the face of it, appear to suggest that a child is consenting. However, the child may have very little understanding about what she is saying yes to. For example:

> Andrew was 15 when he sexually abused Gemma, his seven-year-old cousin for whom he used to baby-sit. Andrew knew that what he was doing was wrong but he asked Gemma 'shall we play the sex game'. Gemma, who used to like playing other games with Andrew said yes, smiling. When caught, Andrew replied that Gemma had agreed to the behaviours and that her smile had shown him that she was excited about it.

There are a number of important elements of consent that you can use when you are trying to make sense of what your child has done. As a general rule, to be able to 'consent' to a sexual act with someone you need to:

- Understand fully what is being asked or suggested to you.
- Not feel pressured into saying 'yes'.
- Know what the behaviour means and what other people might think of it.
- Know what the consequences of going along with the behaviour would be.
- Know that the other person will go along with your decision, regardless of what it is.

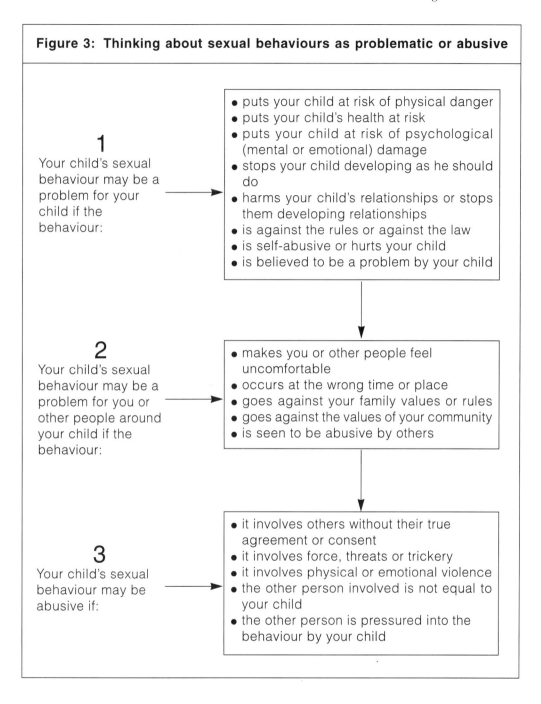

Figure 3: Thinking about sexual behaviours as problematic or abusive

1

Your child's sexual behaviour may be a problem for your child if the behaviour:

- puts your child at risk of physical danger
- puts your child's health at risk
- puts your child at risk of psychological (mental or emotional) damage
- stops your child developing as he should do
- harms your child's relationships or stops them developing relationships
- is against the rules or against the law
- is self-abusive or hurts your child
- is believed to be a problem by your child

2

Your child's sexual behaviour may be a problem for you or other people around your child if the behaviour:

- makes you or other people feel uncomfortable
- occurs at the wrong time or place
- goes against your family values or rules
- goes against the values of your community
- is seen to be abusive by others

3

Your child's sexual behaviour may be abusive if:

- it involves others without their true agreement or consent
- it involves force, threats or trickery
- it involves physical or emotional violence
- the other person involved is not equal to your child
- the other person is pressured into the behaviour by your child

Because of their limited development, children are not able to fully understand the implications of sexual activities and therefore cannot offer real or 'informed' consent. Thinking about Gemma's situation above, Andrew had been a caring person for her who had given her lots of positive attention when he babysat for her. He used to play games with her and spoil her. She had grown to like him and wanted to please him. She had no idea at all what Andrew was suggesting, nor what the consequences of the 'game' would be. Andrew did not threaten or physically force her, but because he was in a position of trust over Gemma, he did not have to. Later, in treatment work, Andrew acknowledged that he would have abused Gemma whether or not she had said 'yes' but that he had deliberately asked her so that he would feel better about what he was doing.

Whilst children and young people do engage in some sexual activities which are normal and not abusive for their age, they can only consent to behaviours that are appropriate for their age, understanding and stage of development. The level of this behaviour changes as children grow and develop. As children mature, it is usually the case that, because they learn more about the meaning of sex and they mature intellectually, socially, emotionally and sexually, they can consent to increasingly sophisticated sexual interactions with others. However, the age and understanding of the child is only one aspect of consent when assessing sexually abusive behaviours. Even where a victim is as old as the young person who is abusing, if the victim was forced or intimidated, true consent cannot be said to have been given. All the following aspects are signs of a child not being able to give consent:

- A child who is **forced, tricked** or **bribed** to go along with a sexual act.
- A child who goes along with something sexual because she is **frightened** or **scared**.
- A child who goes along with some kind of sexual act because she **cannot say 'no'** to the person or because the person is **bigger** or **more powerful**.
- A child who says 'yes' to something she **does not fully understand**.
- A child who is asked directly, 'can I do this' and says 'yes' **but cannot comfortably say 'no'** to the question (because of fear, etc.)

As well as the issue of consent, **power** is a second helpful idea to help us look at whether a sexual behaviour is abusive or not (O'Callaghan and Print, 1994). In most sexual abuse situations the young person who is abusing uses his power to cut back on the ability of the victim to say 'no' or to have a free choice. This power may be because of age, gender, physical strength, the young person's authority over the victim, as in Andrew's case, his position as babysitter, or a difference in level of understanding or intelligence. When considering a sexual act between two children, it is important to weigh up how equal the participants were in relation to all these points.

Myths and facts about sexual abuse by young people

There are a number of powerful myths that surround young people's sexually abusive behaviour and these myths can get in the way of parents' attempts to understand their child's actions. Seeing the truth behind the myth is an important step to better understanding why your child has behaved in this way and what can be done to help. Some of the most common myths are introduced briefly in the following section and are explored in more depth throughout the book.

Myth: Young people don't abuse; they are only experimenting

Fact: It is true that children do experiment with sex and their bodies from an early age and this is a normal and acceptable part of children's development. However, some children and young people go far beyond the boundaries of what is acceptable or normal experimentation and hurt other people, either physically or emotionally, by their sexual behaviour. These behaviours are certainly not part of normal growing up but are sometimes confused as such by parents and professionals.

Myth: Children and young people who sexually abuse others are only repeating their own experiences of being sexually abused. They are acting out what has been done to them or what they have seen

Fact: To understand this issue, it is important to separate children and young people out into different categories.

Firstly, we know that younger children (i.e. those under ten years old) who engage in sexually problematic or abusive behaviours are more likely to have been sexually abused themselves than are teenagers who abuse. The younger the child displaying sexually problematic behaviours, the more likely it is that the child is repeating his own abuse.

Secondly, although the exact figures vary, studies of *young men* (i.e. teenagers) who sexually abuse consistently find that under 50 per cent of such young men have themselves been sexually abused. This suggests that, on its own, experiencing sexual abuse is not a good enough explanation of why a young man might behave in a sexually abusive way. However, most young men who sexually abuse others have experienced some kind of abuse, traumatic experience or severe difficulty in their lives, although this need not be sexual. Indeed, experiencing severe physical abuse appears to be more frequently reported than sexual abuse in the earlier life experiences of young men who sexually abuse (Calder, 2001).

Thirdly, although less is currently known about this area, *girls* who sexually abuse (both younger girls and teenagers) are much more likely to have been sexually abused themselves than boys or young men. Some studies, although only covering small numbers, indicate that nearly 100 per cent of such young women have themselves been subjected to sexual abuse (Calder, 2001).

Myth: Young people only carry out minor forms of sexual abuse

Fact: Information from studies and from professionals working with young people who abuse suggests clearly that young people show a full range of sexually abusive behaviours from 'non-contact offences' (where the abuser does not touch the victim, such as indecent exposure or 'flashing') to rape. Again, studies vary depending on whether the young people concerned have been convicted, are in custody or live in the community. In one study of young British male abusers, 54 per cent had penetrated their victims and 68 per cent had used physical force against their victims (Richardson, Graham and Bhate, 1995). In two other UK studies, between 20 per cent (Monck and New, 1996) and 29 per cent (Beckett and Brown, forthcoming) of young people had penetrated their victims, but most of the young people had perpetrated non-penetrative but contact abuse, such as forcing the victim to touch and masturbate them, oral sex, attempts to penetrate, etc. Accounts from survivors who were abused by adolescents highlight how painful and damaging sexual abuse can be, irrespective of the age of the abuser. The message from survivors is that we should take a young person's sexually abusive behaviour just as seriously as that of an adult.

Myth: If a young person has abused once, he is unlikely to do it again

Fact: We know that for some young people who sexually abuse, the sexually abusive behaviour can become highly addictive and virtually impossible for them to stop by themselves without involvement and help from other people. Chapter 3 explores this in more detail. It is now recognised that some young people may be less likely to abuse again than others. This probably has something to do both with the quality of the work done with them and with how many other positive attributes they have in their lives. At the moment, it is difficult for professionals to accurately assess which specific children are likely to stop abusing. There are two crucial messages from this. The first is the importance of offering help and support as soon as possible to all young people who have abused to try to stop them becoming 'hooked on' the feelings created by the abuse. We know that children and young people who receive such help (from professionals and families) are less likely to carry on abusing. Secondly, by adding and encouraging positive or protective factors, parents can directly contribute to a reduction in the likelihood of further abuse by their child.

Myth: Young people don't plan or think in advance about abusing, they just do it.

Fact: When asked about this, most young people say at first that they did not plan the abuse, but just acted on the spur of the moment and ended up abusing. However, professionals think that sexually abusive behaviour rarely happens spontaneously or without advanced planning. Most young people who sexually abuse do so having thought about the abuse for some time beforehand, having made efforts to set up the situation, having imagined what it would be like and having attempted to gain the victim's trust or compliance. These issues are explored in more detail in Chapter 3.

Myth: Young people don't know that what they are doing is wrong.

Fact: For some young people this is true as they seem not to have developed a sense of knowing what is right or wrong sexually or they have received messages as younger children that it is OK to act in a sexually abusive way. However, most young people who abuse do know on some level that what they are doing is wrong, although in many cases they try to convince themselves that their actions are acceptable and not harmful. This is usually to try to make themselves feel better and justify their actions. Some young people use drugs or alcohol as a way of doing this. Other young people know very clearly that it is wrong to abuse, but this knowledge alone is not enough for them to stop themselves, as the sexual feelings they gain from abusing are so powerful. The younger the child, of course, the more likely it is that he is not aware of the full implications of the sexual behaviour, although many younger children who engage in sexually inappropriate behaviours know that these would be viewed as 'naughty' or 'dirty' or 'bad'.

As a guide, remember that most young people who abuse do so in secrecy and take steps to make sure they are not seen or caught. Of course, this shows that, on some level, they know the behaviours would be frowned upon or seen as wrong if they were discovered. Regardless of how much they know that abuse is wrong, few young people who abuse really fully understand the consequences of their actions for their victims.

Myth: It is rare for young people to sexually abuse.

Fact: Sexual abuse by children and young people accounts for approximately 25–33 per cent of all sexual abuse committed in the UK (Erooga and Masson, 1999). When it hits the headlines, there is usually shock and anger that a 'child' could have behaved in this way, but it is nevertheless true that young people are responsible for a significant amount of all sexual abuse committed. Indeed, a recent NSPCC study found that more people in a random sample of adults said that they had been sexually abused by brothers or step-brothers when they were children than by their fathers or step-fathers (NSPCC, 2000).

Whilst this suggests that sexual abuse by children and young people makes up a significant amount of all sexual abuse, it is important to bear in mind that the vast majority of children and young people in the whole population do not sexually abuse, irrespective of difficulties in their lives.

Summary points from this section

- Children and young people's sexual behaviour may be normal and appropriate, problematic or abusive.
- Sexually abusive behaviour takes many forms, but it can be distinguished from normal behaviour because there is a victim who is used and hurt as a result.
- If we are thinking about sexual interactions between children and young people it is important to see beyond the behaviour itself and to look closely into the circumstances of what went on, from different points of view—not just the child's but also from the victim's perspective.
- Examining children and young people's sexual behaviour in relation to issues of 'consent' and 'power' can help us to understand the abusive element of the behaviour.
- There are many myths associated with young people's sexually abusive behaviours. It is important to take abuse seriously and to learn the truth about sexual abuse by young people in order to help your child.

Questions to consider

- What do you know of the wider circumstances beyond the sexual activities that your child was involved in?
- Can you distinguish the separate parts of your child's sexual behaviour and position them along the 'normal–abusive' continuum, so that you can see what is the most concerning?
- Can you work out what is problematic (why and for whom) and what is abusive (why)?
- Can you identify any 'myths' or misconceptions about sexual abuse that have influenced the way you have understood or responded to your child's behaviour?

Exercise 2: Thinking about your child's sexual behaviours

Purpose. This exercise provides you with an opportunity to consider your child's sexual behaviours on a continuum and to separate out those behaviours that are abusive from others that are OK.

1. Think about each of the sexual behaviours you know, or understand, your child has been involved in. Mark a cross on the line where you would put each behaviour, number it and briefly describe it in the corresponding section below:

Clearly OK	Somewhere in the middle: the grey area	Clearly not OK: abusive
Normal for the age of my child	Not sure: could be normal or not normal, depending on certain things…	Not normal for the age of my child

2. When you have listed each of the sexual behaviours you know your child has been involved in, look at each of the three sections as a whole and try to work out what is different about the behaviours you have put in the three sections. (NB You may feel that all your child's sexual behaviours fit in one category).

3. For any behaviours listed in the 'grey area', think about what else you would need to know that would help you make a decision either way about the behaviour, e.g. more information about power or consent, etc.

Exercise 3: Checklist to assess your child's sexual behaviours

Purpose. This exercise gives you an opportunity to review why and to whom your child's sexual behaviour is problematic or abusive.

1. Think carefully about the particular sexual behaviour which has been brought to your attention. Try to establish why and to whom the behaviour is problematic by answering all of the questions below:

1.1 Is my child's sexual behaviour a problem for my child?	Yes	No	Don't know
Does the behaviour put my child in physical danger?			
Is there a health risk for my child?			
Is there a risk that my child will be psychologically (mentally or emotionally) damaged?			
Is the behaviour stopping my child from developing as they should?			
Does the behaviour get in the way of my child making normal relationships?			
Is my child's behaviour against the rules or against the law?			
Is my child's behaviour self-abusive or does it hurt them?			
Does my child believe that the behaviour is a problem?			

1.2 Is my child's sexual behaviour a problem for other people:	Yes	No	Don't know
Does my child's sexual behaviour make other people feel uncomfortable?			
Does my child's sexual behaviour occur at the wrong time?			
Does my child's sexual behaviour occur in the wrong place?			
Does my child's behaviour conflict with the rules in my family?			
Does it conflict with the rules of the community?			
Are other people judging my child's behaviour to be abusive?			

1.3 Is my child's sexual behaviour abusive?	Yes	No	Don't know
Did my child involve someone else in the sexual behaviour who didn't or couldn't give their full consent?			
Did the others involved in the situation have an equal say in what happened? Did they have equal power?			
Was any physical or emotional pressure put on one of those involved to take part?			
Were any threats or force used or was there any aggression?			

2. Look back at your answers above and summarise what you have found out by completing the following statements:

2.1 My child's sexual behaviour is a problem for my child because...

....

....

....

....

2.2 My child's sexual behaviour is a problem for me because...

....

....

....

....

2.3 My child's sexual behaviour is a problem for other people because...

....

....

....

....

2.4 My child's sexual behaviour is abusive because...

....

....

....

....

Thinking about the Consequences of Sexual Abuse and the Victim's Experiences

When trying to balance the needs of the young person who has abused, other people in your family and your own needs, thinking about the consequences of your child's sexually abusive behaviour for the victim may be the last thing you wish to face. However, it is important to remember when dealing with the sexual abuse that there was a victim, someone who has in some way been damaged or hurt by the behaviour. The victim may be unknown to you, acquainted with you or in some cases, your child too. Chapter 2 goes into more detail about how to respond if the victim is also your child.

Learning about how best to stop sexually abusive behaviour requires 'clear thinking' about victims. By this I mean that it is important to deal with your child in a way which would be respectful to the victim concerned. This is a principle I apply in my work with young people who abuse. For example, when I am listening to a young person talking about his behaviour, I may consciously ask myself 'would this statement be acceptable for the victim of the abuse?' 'Clear thinking' about victims for parents means making sure that you do not automatically jump in on the side of your child (or believe your child's accounts over the victim's) just because one child is yours and the other is not. Try to bear in mind the following points about victims:

- Victims may not show any outward signs of distress, especially if they are very young. This does not mean that the abuse was insignificant to them, nor that they have simply 'got over' the abuse.

- Victims do not just forget what has happened. Many adults who have experienced abuse as small children still struggle with the consequences of the abuse many years after the abuse itself has stopped. (If you need help because you have experienced sexual abuse as a child, see Chapter 4).

- Young people who sexually abuse frequently try to justify and minimise their behaviour by making out that the victim encouraged them, gave them 'consent' or enjoyed what happened.

It is not only important for you as a parent to retain a level of 'clear thinking' about victims, but it is also necessary to respond appropriately if your child suggests or says something which is not respectful of the victim, or which tries to minimise his actions. If this happens, it is important to gently but firmly let your child know that you disagree and offer a correction to the incorrect statement.

Who are the victims of young people's sexual abuse?

Young people abuse a wide range of victims. There is no one type of victim, just as there is not one kind of abusive act. It is important to view each situation as unique and to see the victim as an individual who was in some way made vulnerable and hurt by the young person who abused. Occasionally, parents have questioned how a victim they know to have been tough or 'streetwise' could have allowed the abuse to happen. Again, 'clear thinking' about victims recognises that just because a child appears to be assertive in one setting, does not mean that she could stop the abuse.

It is most common for young people to know their victims, either as siblings in families, or neighbours or children they know in the local community. Victims can be any age, from babies to old people, and may even be animals. Most frequently though, young people abuse younger children. The majority of victims of teenagers are under ten and the average age quoted in several studies is around six or seven years old (Ryan, Miyoshi, Metzner, Krugman and Fryer, 1996; Johnson, 1988). It is common for young people to have abused on many occasions and have a number of victims. One study (Abel, Rouleau and Cunningham-Rathner, 1986) noted that the average juvenile sex offender had committed eight sexual offences and victimised an average of six people.

Young people can abuse either males or females or both. Approximately a quarter of young people abuse only male victims, slightly less than a half abuse only female victims and between a quarter to a third appear to have victims of both genders (Calder, 2001). Often a young person's choice of gender is not related to his future sexuality. Some young men who abuse boys develop into adults who are heterosexual. Some young men abuse girls but develop into adults who are gay. It is less common for young people to abuse people of their own age or adults. When they do, it is most common for young men to abuse young women.

What do victims need?

A proportion of young people who have sexually abused, just like some adults who sexually offend, will try to make out that they have not harmed their victims. Some young people have actually convinced themselves of this. It is known, however, that experiencing sexual abuse is a very painful experience which can have long-lasting effects on the victim. It is known that the psychological damage done to the victim is the hardest aspect of the abuse to recover from.

As a parent you cannot undo or take away the victim's experience of being abused. However, if a child is believed when she talks of being abused, if the child is protected and cared for after the abuse, then she can recover. If victims are blamed or made to feel responsible, then the damage is likely to be increased. As parents therefore, you can have an impact on the victim by making sure that the responsibility for the abuse is placed on the abuser and that the victim is not left in a risky or unsafe position.

Due to the dynamics of their relationship with the abuser, and because they have often been silenced or made to feel guilty during the abuse, it can be difficult for victims to find the words to express their true feelings or opinions. Younger children in particular can struggle to put feelings into words. This means that it is absolutely vital not to put pressure on victims of abuse to accept the young person back into the family. For example, a child who was abused by her brother is asked whether she would like to see him may very well find it impossible to answer 'No'. This emphasises how important it is firstly to put safety measures in place to limit or stop the young person's contact with any victims (see Chapter 5) and secondly to offer the victim support (sometimes therapy) to help overcome the experience of being abused.

Summary points from this section

- Sexually abusive behaviour has damaging consequences both for the victim and the young person who is abusing.
- Victims should be respected and protected by parents and professionals who are trying to help the young person who has abused.
- Because of what happens in relationships where a child is abused, victims should not be put in a position where they have to make pressured decisions about contact or rehabilitation with a sibling who has abused them. Victims need protecting first and foremost.

Questions to consider

- Is your child attempting to put the blame on the victim in any way?
- Are there ways in which you could respond which would better respect the victim's experience?

Understanding What is and what isn't Normal in Children and Young People's Sexual Behaviour

Parents often say that they lose confidence in being able to make decisions about what is and is not normal sexual behaviour after their child has sexually abused. I have drawn up (from the work of Ryan, Johnson, Hanks, in Calder, 2001, and others) the following section on childhood sexual behaviours as a guide for parents . Although the focus of the book is young people who have sexually abused, I also include some ideas about younger children's sexual behaviours. This may help you to look back and reassess the sexual behaviours that your adolescent engaged in earlier in his life, or it may help you to assess the sexual behaviours of any younger children you have.

Children's sexual development can be considered in two main phases and four categories, as shown here:

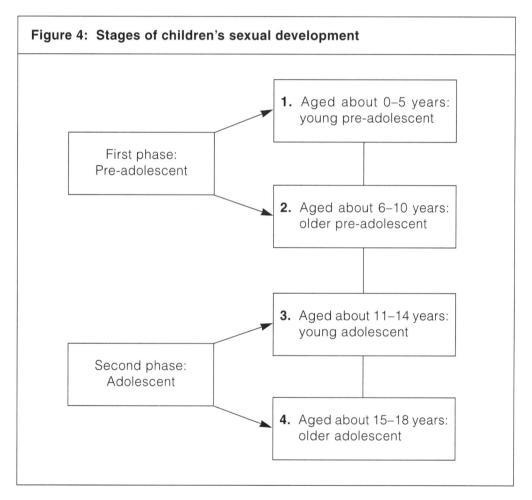

Figure 4: Stages of children's sexual development

First phase:
Pre-adolescent

1. Aged about 0–5 years: young pre-adolescent

2. Aged about 6–10 years: older pre-adolescent

Second phase:
Adolescent

3. Aged about 11–14 years: young adolescent

4. Aged about 15–18 years: older adolescent

There are two reasons to be cautious about these stages. Firstly, children develop physically and sexually at different rates. The behaviours and the corresponding ages suggested should be seen as a guide only, rather than being fixed. Secondly, as seen above, it is not enough to think only about the behaviour itself, but it is necessary to place sexual behaviour in its context and to look into the exact circumstances in which the sexual behaviours occur. A sexual behaviour that would seem acceptable in one setting may be completely inappropriate in another. Therefore, when trying to apply the ideas in this section to your own child's behaviour, you should consider not only your own child's age and developmental level, but also the age and the development of the other child involved and the age difference, ability, power and consent issues between them.

Normal sexual behaviour in pre-adolescents

Stage one: children aged up to five years old (young pre-adolescents)

From an early age, children explore their own bodies and those of other young children. Very young children from approximately aged two years old (both boys and girls) may touch their own sexual parts and stimulate themselves. For example, they can rub themselves when going to sleep and they experience pleasure from this. Whilst such behaviour should be neither actively encouraged nor ignored by parents, it is important to recognise it as normal and not give children an impression that they are 'naughty' or 'dirty' for behaving in this way. Stressing to children that they should touch themselves only when they are alone and in a safe place is the correct way to respond.

From the age of around two to four years old children may show an interest in looking at the genitals of other children, as well as touching their own and other children's bodies, usually within play and games, e.g. 'you show me yours, I'll show you mine' or 'doctors and nurses'. They do these things with children of the same age, size and stage of development. These are normal behaviours and expressions of the child's curiosity and desire to explore. There is no pressure on any of the children involved. Such behaviours do not take up a large amount of time for the child. They usually happen away from the eyes of adults, are not planned in advance and can be light-hearted, e.g. accompanied by giggling, etc. Parents discovering these behaviours should put some boundaries around the behaviours and gently discourage them. As a result the child learns some important messages about when and when not to behave in this way, the importance of privacy in respect of their own bodies and touch. In normal circumstances, all of the above behaviours can be easily distracted by an adult directing the child or children onto another activity. If a child shows that she is worried, scared or afraid, shameful or angry at this age about any touching behaviour, then this is a sign that all is not right.

During this stage of development it is also common for children to ask questions of their parents or carers about where babies come from. You should give brief but truthful answers to children's questions in a de-personalised way, for example, 'babies come from their mummy's tummies…' Children will usually be satisfied with basic mechanical facts about babies and childbirth. This does not encourage them to try out behaviours, nor does it damage them in any way. As they get older, children begin to know more about body differences between males and females and can name body parts with increasing accuracy. You can help by teaching proper, but age-appropriate names for body parts.

Towards the end of this stage, as children begin to pick up messages from other people, they can become more shy and embarrassed about bodies and sex. At this point children may demand privacy, although they may remain extremely interested in the toilet or bathroom activities of others.

Despite all of the above activities which are a part of normal sexual development for young children, children of this age have little understanding of adult sex and the ways adults express their sexuality, nor do they need this information at this point.

Stage two: children aged six to ten years old (older pre-adolescents)

Children at this point in their development are normally becoming more aware of sexuality through the influence of TV and discussion with friends, including 'playground talk' which can lead to a good deal of confusion and misinformation. Children's outward attitude (for example, to seeing people kissing on TV) may be 'Yak!' and they may show some embarrassment about sexual matters, nevertheless they can be quite interested in such things.

Masturbation in private and exploration of bodies with other children are common at five and six years of age. Children are also aware that touching feels good. At around the age of five to eight years, children's questions change to the how and why, for example 'how does a man put his willy in a woman?' or 'why do people like doing sex?' At this stage children tend to spend most time with children of the same gender, although they can talk of having 'boyfriends' and 'girlfriends' and play sex games at school, e.g. 'kiss-catch' etc.

From about the age of seven or eight there tends to be a natural decrease in how often children explore each other's bodies. However, as they grow through this stage, changes in hormones are already taking place in a child's body, in preparation for full puberty which happens later. These changes mean that, for the first time, children can be sexually attracted to others around them, although at this point this does not lead to sexual arousal or intimate sexual activities.

Towards the end of this stage some children are already entering into full puberty, so it is vital that children from eight or nine years have complete information about body changes, etc. It is appropriate to give children at this age information using simple and accurate terms, to stress that body parts or functions are not dirty and that the children should respect their own bodies as well as others. It is important not to give children inaccurate or confusing messages that they will need to 'unlearn' at a later date.

What is abnormal and concerning in pre-adolescents' sexual behaviours?

For children in both of the above age groups i.e. children up to ten years old, there are certain behaviours which are not normally found in normal exploration and normal sexual development. The more the following points (adapted from Johnson, 1994) apply to a child's behaviours, the more concerned you should be:

- If the children involved in the sexual activity are not usually friends and don't usually play together.
- If the children involved are at different stages of development or different ages.
- If a child seems to have too much sexual knowledge and seems to behave like an adult would about sex.
- If the sexual behaviours are very different to those of other children of the same age.
- If a child does not seem to be able to stop himself doing sexual things or carries on despite being told not to by a parent.
- If a child directs sexual behaviours towards adults.
- If the child's sexual behaviours lead to complaints by other children.
- If the child does, or tries to do, anything sexual with an animal.
- If children's sexual behaviours happen in public.
- If the sexual behaviour involves any kind of threat or if anger is used to make another child go along with it.
- If the child inserts objects into the body of another child.
- If any of the sexual behaviours appear to involve shame, anxiety and guilt.

(Johnson,1994)

Normal sexual behaviour in adolescents

Adolescence is a time when young people's interest and involvement in sex grows strongly. Whilst young people's bodies increasingly make them physically able to engage in sexual activity, these changes often raise parents' concerns about their child's readiness and maturity for such behaviours. Changes in society have also led to different standards around sex now than in previous generations. For example, fewer than 1 per cent of women now aged 55 and over report having had sexual intercourse before the age of sixteen, whereas for today's teenage girls this is 20 per cent (Messer and Jones, 1999). The evidence therefore suggests that today's adolescents engage in more advanced sexual activities at an earlier age than was the case 20 or 30 years ago. This in itself is not necessarily a problem as long as the behaviours are *consenting*, in the young people's *control*, *safe* and *enjoyable* to all taking part.

Stage three: young people aged ten to fourteen years old (young adolescents)

Young people in this age range generally enter full puberty when their bodies develop sexually. The average age for this in Western cultures is now about ten and three quarter years for young women and eleven and a half for young men (Herdt and McClintock, 2000). For young women, the visible and invisible changes associated with puberty typically begin between age nine and thirteen with growth, development of breasts and pubic hair and with periods. Menstruation begins on average at age thirteen but it is normal if this happens anywhere between eleven and a half and fifteen and a half years old. Visible signs of full puberty for young men include the penis and testicles becoming larger and the ability to ejaculate. Whilst the average for this in young men is eleven and a half, anytime between nine and fifteen should be considered normal. With so many changes happening to their bodies and in their minds, young people can often be confused or frightened about sexual matters. This can be especially true if they have not been properly educated about sex before these major body changes take place. Adolescents are easily influenced by their peers and often find it embarrassing and difficult to ask for advice or guidance from their parents about sex.

From around age thirteen, masturbation increases and is accompanied by sexual fantasies. Masturbation is frequent, especially among males. Young people of both sexes can reach orgasm. Sexual attraction to the opposite sex or the same sex becomes stronger. Young people become more conscious of their appearance and dress and they begin to have girlfriend or boyfriend relationships which involve sexual behaviours, from kissing, to touching and, in some cases, to full sex. Parents can help their children through this difficult stage by reassuring them that they are normal and by offering information and support in a relaxed and non-threatening way. You should offer clear information to help your adolescent make sense of confusing messages from other teenagers about sex and to help him understand the possible consequences of sex.

Stage four: young people aged fourteen to eighteen years old (older adolescents)

As they progress through this stage, young people are becoming young adults, both emotionally and socially, although they are easily influenced by media and peer pressure. A high proportion of young people in this age band are involved in consensual sexual activities with other young people. During this stage approximately 50 per cent of adolescents are sexually experienced or active. Young people can find themselves preoccupied by sex for long periods of time. They may also end up involved in sexual activities that they had not anticipated, planned or thought through properly. Their abilities to think clearly and keep control of situations may also be underdeveloped. Within this age range it is normal for young people to:

- Talk in a sexual way to friends and other young people of his or her own age.
- Use sexual swear words and make sexual jokes.
- Be interested in erotic material and use this to masturbate.
- Have boyfriend or girlfriend relationships, which may be stable and longer-term, or may be a series of one-night stands.
- Do sexual things which are consenting, including kissing, fondling, touching genitals, etc.
- Masturbate a boyfriend or girlfriend and have this done to them.
- Have consenting sexual intercourse with people around the same age.

Despite the frequency and normality of such behaviours, young people of this age can still feel uncertain, confused or worried about sex. They can worry about whether their bodies are 'good enough', whether they have normal thoughts and whether they are normal because they masturbate. It is also common for young people to be concerned or embarrassed about not being as experienced sexually as other young people of the same age. If you confront your child at this stage about sex, he is likely to become defensive and secretive. The most important thing you can do at this stage is to help your child make the right kind of choices, with an emphasis on safety. The following pointers, derived from a study of young people's first sexual intercourse experiences (Mitchell and Wellings, 1998), hold true as general sexual goals in relation to teenagers in this age band:

- Sex should be anticipated: not come as a shock to a young person.
- Sex should be wanted (both people concerned should be ready to have sex and should make a joint positive decision to have sex).
- Sex should be safe and protected (both against pregnancy and sexually transmitted diseases).
- Sex should be enjoyed and viewed as a positive and enjoyable experience by both young people.

Although your automatic reaction may be to want to stop your teenager from having non-abusive sex, this is very difficult. Instead, it may be more important to make sure that all the conditions above are met.

The British National Survey of Sexual Attitudes and Lifestyles (Wellings *et al.*, 1994) was carried out between May 1990 and November 1991 and involved interviews with over 18,000 men and women in Britain aged between 16–59 years and provided an opportunity to explore sexual behaviours of young people. The study found that:

- Both men and women are now sexually active at earlier ages than in previous generations. Over the last 40 years there has been a steady reduction in the age at which young people have sexual intercourse for the first time. The most common age for young people to have full sex is now 17.
- The earlier young men and women begin sexual activity, the higher the chances are that they will have a child in their teens. Teenagers who have intercourse before the age of 16 are four times more likely to become parents before age 20 than those who delay sexual activity until later. It is not that early sex is the problem in itself, but a lack of sex education, lack of planning and failure to use contraceptives.
- Talking about sex with parents helps protect young women from early pregnancies. The study found that young women from families in which there was no discussion about sexual matters were more than twice as likely to have become mothers in their teens than those from families who discussed sex easily.

- Young people's attitudes towards teenage sexual activity are strongly affected by the family environment in which they live and the attitudes held by parents.

Taken together, this means that young people are now sexually active for much longer periods before becoming parents. As parents, we should encourage our teenage children to make appropriate and safe choices about sex. We can help them in this by ensuring that they have accurate information and sex education and that they feel supported by us in all aspects of their lives.

What is abnormal and concerning in adolescents' sexual behaviours?

Because it is normal for many adolescents to engage in intimate sexual behaviours, it can be more difficult to think about what might be abnormal in this age band. Sometimes, the context (who was involved, how they came to the decision, how they felt, etc.) is a better indicator of abnormal or problematic sexuality in adolescents than the nature of the sexual act itself. However, some warning signs (derived from Ryan and Lane, 1991; and Ryan *et al.*, 1996) include:

- A young person who does sexual things indiscriminately (i.e. makes no distinction about when, where, who with, etc.) or compulsively (i.e. cannot stop himself).
- A young person who sees violence or aggression as an acceptable part of sex.
- A young person who indecently exposes (flashes) himself, rubs himself against other people sexually or makes sexually obscene telephone calls.
- A young person who cannot seem to stop masturbating, especially if this gets in the way of doing other day-to-day tasks or if it is in public.
- A young person who tries to expose children's genitals by pulling down their clothing especially if this carries on when the young person has been warned or if it involves physical aggression or force.
- A young person who uses pornography which shows people hurting each other, violence or children.
- A young person who has sexual conversations or sexual contact with younger children.
- A young person who tries to, or succeeds in, touching another person's genitals without permission.
- A young person who makes sexual threats to someone.
- A young person who forces someone into sex, sexual assaults or rapes someone, regardless of the age of the victim.
- A young person who has any sexual contact with animals.

Sexual Development and Sexually Abusive Behaviour in Young People who have Learning Disabilities

A proportion of young people who sexually abuse have a degree of learning disability: in other words they have what used to be called a mental impairment or handicap. Learning disability is an 'umbrella term' for many different conditions, some of which have only minor implications for a child's sexual development, though others may have wide-ranging consequences. Like young people who are not disabled, young people with learning disabilities are individuals who have a range of needs and experiences. Sex is just as important to such young people as it is to other teenagers.

When young people with a learning disability sexually abuse it is sometimes assumed that the sexually abusive behaviour is naïve and has happened just because they do not know what is normal and acceptable sexual behaviour or because they are sexually frustrated. Young people with learning disabilities have traditionally been given less sex education than young people who are not disabled and they are, if anything, even more vulnerable than non-disabled children to being sexually abused themselves. They may abuse for the same range of reasons and they may show the same range of sexually abusive behaviours as other young people. Their sexually abusive behaviour is no more or less damaging to victims than that of young people who do not have such disabilities. We need to treat it just as seriously and our attempts to support and help such children and to protect others are just as important as with all young people who abuse. At the same time, differentiating what is and is not abusive may be more difficult for parents and professionals in respect of young people with learning disabilities as issues of consent may be harder to work out. Some sexual behaviours in young people with learning disabilities would be better labelled as sexually problematic or inappropriate behaviour; for example, a young learning-disabled man who exposes his penis in public in front of a group of children may have never been taught that this is not appropriate.

Some parents have assumed that sexual development is not an issue because of the 'mental age' of their child. However, while young people with learning disabilities may not be as advanced in their thinking, they may develop sexually at the same age as other young people without learning disabilities. Parents may worry that the child's sexual development is out of step with his or her ability to make decisions and appropriate sexual choices. As a result, they may discourage their child from any form of sexual activity and not offer sex education. However, if the sexuality of a young person with learning disabilities is repressed or squashed, this is more likely to encourage secretive and abusive acts which compensate for the child's lack of sex education and opportunities to have consensual sex. There is a need to give young people with learning disabilities the right kind of information and opportunities at the correct time so that their sexuality becomes a positive and important part of their adolescence, as it should be for all young people. Therefore, the major tasks, as far as sexuality is concerned, for parents whose child has a learning disability include:

- Making sure the child has all the sex education she needs in a way which she can properly understand in order to help make sense of body changes, sexual feelings and relationships.

- Giving assistance in learning what is acceptable and not acceptable sexually, correct places for sexual expression, etc.

- Protecting the child from abuse and harm from others who may try to coerce the young person into behaviours she does not fully understand.

- Offering the child appropriate opportunities to develop self esteem, as well as positive and non-abusive social and sexual relationships.

Summary points from this section

- From an early age children do explore their sexuality and show sexual behaviours.
- What is normal and not normal may be different for your children than it was for you when you were a child.
- Young people now are doing more sexual things at an earlier age than was the case several decades ago.
- Parents need to understand what is normal at different ages and be able to keep things in perspective, so that they can respond properly to their child.

Questions to consider

- How do your own experiences inform your values about sex and childhood sexuality? How similar or different are your thoughts from those presented in this chapter?
- How did other people respond to your sexuality when you were growing up and how did this help or hinder your development?
- What do you need to do to ensure that your children are adequately protected from abusive sex but are free enough to develop normal and healthy sexual interests?

Exercise 4: Thinking about when sexual behaviours are normal

Purpose. This exercise gives you an opportunity to think about what sexual behaviours you consider to be normal and at what ages.

1. Think about the sexual behaviours listed below. Assume that all the people involved are of the same age and that no one is being forced at all. At what age do you think that these behaviours are normal and OK? Write the age in the boxes on the left.

OK age to do this   Sexual behaviour

Hugging

Kissing

Masturbation alone

Two children touching each other's sexual parts over clothes

Two children touching each other's sexual parts under clothes

Two children masturbating each other

Two children having oral sex

Two children having sexual intercourse (full sex)

2. Look back at your answers. How would your answers change if you imagine two young people of the same sex doing these things?

....

....

....

....

....

....

....

3. If you are a single carer, ask a friend who you trust to fill in this form separately from you. If you share the care of a young person with a partner, ask your partner to fill it in. Either way, share your answers with the other person and discuss the reasons behind your choices. Pay particular attention to any answers that are very different between the two people. Why have you got such different answers?

....

....

....

....

....

....

4. Would your answers change if you repeat the exercise thinking only about your child who has sexually abused? If you could ensure that your child was with a consenting partner and that the behaviours were non-abusive, how many of the above behaviours would you feel comfortable with your child taking part in?

....

....

....

....

....

....

Chapter 2
Finding out

Dealing with Finding out
What to do, who to tell and why

For most parents who are reading this book, the abuse will already have come to light and professionals (usually a social worker, police officer, probation officer or psychologist) will be involved. It is possible however, that some parents will have found out about the abuse and have kept their knowledge of it within the family. If this is the case, it is very important to seek the help of a professional. You should start by contacting your local social services department and talking to a social worker, usually a duty officer, who will be able to advise you. You should be prepared to give your name and details of your family, even though you may be worried about doing this. At the same time, you need to be aware of the consequences of reporting the abuse.

The social worker will most probably want to gather as much information from you about what you have seen or been told. She will then need to go and talk to other professionals, like the police and any health visitor involved in your family. The social worker will ask you your name and will need to speak to the police about the behaviours. There will be a first meeting where all the professionals come together and a plan will be made about how best to move the situation on. Following this, it is likely that a social worker and a police officer will want to talk to you and the young person who has been displaying the sexually abusive behaviour. Mostly this is done in a specialist centre where the interview with your child will be video recorded. This is very stressful for families, but you should be able to go along with your child to the centre, although usually you will not be allowed in the room. Depending on what your child says, he may be charged with an offence and may need to go to court. (See Chapter 6 for more details of the Child Protection and Criminal Justice Systems.)

Whilst informing the authorities about your child is a stressful and difficult thing to do, it is the only way in the long-term that you can be sure that you can help your child. There may be many arguments going around your head as to whether you should or should not tell. If you are in a relationship, you and your partner may disagree about what to do. Whilst there are no easy ways forward, it is important that the young person is faced with the consequences of his actions. If a parent keeps the information inside the family, the young person is likely to feel that his behaviour is not a big deal or that the abuse is not being taken seriously. Here are some of the arguments against informing a professional or the authorities of the abuse and the corresponding benefits to be gained by telling:

Reasons for keeping abuse to self	Benefits of telling or informing authorities
✗ 'I'm too scared'	✔ Whilst the fear is real, not telling is likely to increase your fear of the future in the long run. You can't run away from the problem
✗ 'I should be able to handle this myself'	✔ Parents shouldn't have to cope with such an enormous problem alone. Treating children and young people with such problems is a specialist area. There is no reason why a parent should be able to do this alone.
✗ 'I want to help my child myself'	✔ You will still have an opportunity to help. Indeed, your role will be absolutely crucial. But, telling is the only way you will get help (for yourself and for your child) and ensure that the victim is protected.
✗ 'My child has promised me it won't happen again'	✔ Young people often need to experience the consequences of their actions. Whilst they promise it won't reoccur, such behaviours often don't just vanish.
✗ 'My child might get in trouble, be sent away or even to prison	✔ You cannot know for sure what will happen to your child as a result of informing the authorities, but a criminal offence may have been committed and it is important to act.

How should I feel on finding out about the abuse?

Because of the secrecy and stigma attached to sexual abuse, you are unlikely to meet other parents in the same situation as you unless you are involved in a group where there are other parents whose children have sexually abused. Unfortunately, not all projects working in this field have enough resources to offer such groups to parents. Even if you can talk to friends and other family members about what you are facing, they may not fully appreciate your position. Some parents tell other people they trust about the abuse, only to find that they are rejected or, sometimes even worse, that information they had passed on in confidence is then spread within their neighbourhood or wider family.

When they first find out about the abuse, parents often feel a horrible mixture of shock, anger, denial, confusion, guilt, isolation and helplessness. Although there is no single way you should feel, many of these feelings come naturally from the overwhelming and difficult situation that you are in. You should remember that there are other parents in your position who are experiencing similar feelings, though you may never meet them. You can expect to have some days that are better than others, but lots of the time you may feel down and depressed. You may find yourself with thoughts of the abuse or intrusive pictures in your head about what you know has happened or, sometimes even worse, disturbing fantasies about what you imagine might have happened.

The discovery of the abuse is often a crushing blow to parents. It can shatter your sense of certainty and normality. Faced with this, some parents deny all or some of the information they have been given and want to pull the whole family closer and 'make it all better again'. Others feel that they are not able to take care of the conflicting needs of victim and abuser, particularly if they are both within the same family. Parents may be forced into making choices that are seemingly impossible, for example, having to choose who remains living at home.

What have other parents said about discovering that their child has sexually abused?

In the following section I attempt to represent some of the common feelings that parents have reported to me when discussing their feelings after having found out about the abuse. Whilst some of these feelings may be particularly strong in the early stages, parents have explained that these feelings can stay with them for long periods of time. I also offer some ideas about how to deal with these feelings, again based on what other parents have told me has helped them.

Feeling like a failure as a parent

All parents who are faced with their child's problem behaviours can feel like failures or wonder what they might have done to 'create' a child with such behaviours. This feeling can be particularly strong when the behaviours in question are sexually abusive ones. Time after time parents have talked to me about how the discovery of their child's abusive behaviour has left them feeling like a total failure as a parent. Parents who have not abused their children, especially fathers, have talked of how they feel that other people, both friends and professionals, regard them with suspicion, as if they must have sexually abused their children for this behaviour to have emerged.

The sense of failure as a parent may also be particularly strong if you are the parent of one child who has abused another of your children. In such cases, you have to face not only the fact that one of your children has been abused and victimised, and confront the feelings of anger and guilt that this brings, but also the feeling that you have been responsible for raising the child who has abused. Parents can feel that they have failed both children and that they must therefore be 'bad' or 'useless' as parents. Often mothers feel an acute sense of failure because being a mother is so frequently seen as being about protecting and bringing up children. It is not fair for either parent to be left with these feelings in isolation from the other.

Shock and denial

It is very common for parents to be so shocked by their child's behaviour that they find themselves denying either *all* or *part* of what has taken place. Some parents question whether the abuse happened at all or claim that there must have been a misunderstanding. Most parents, however, recognise that there is a problem, even if they still cannot quite believe everything. Sometimes, parents can only cope with the horror of the abuse by facing and accepting bits of information at a time.

Guilt, shame and blame

Linked to the shock and denial, parents often express feelings of guilt in relation to having been responsible for the abuser at the time of the abuse. It is common for parents to struggle with the questions 'should I or could I have known?' and 'was it my fault?' Some parents express anger at themselves, their partner or the young person who has abused. Anger can sometimes become directed to the wrong person, such as to the victim: 'why didn't you tell me that this was happening?' or to a partner: 'you were there at the time, why didn't you notice?' or 'if you hadn't lost your temper all the time or been away such a lot, then this wouldn't have happened!'

Being able to express the guilt and shame you are feeling can be an important step. If you keep these feelings to yourself then there is a risk that they will 'eat away' inside you. Being able to share them can help correct any errors you have in misplacing responsibility for the abuse. The exercise later in this chapter on responsibility issues is designed to help with this.

Isolation and stigma

One of the most striking things I have learnt by working in groups with parents of children who have sexually abused, is the extent of the isolation and loneliness that parents and families can face after the abuse has come to light. Parents often find themselves living in fear of other family and community members learning about the abuse. They understand that if others in the community were to find out, their children and homes could be at risk. Unfortunately, some families are forced to move or to go into hiding because of the consequences of other people in the community finding out about what has happened. Even if you are able to make sure that the information about the abuse is only given to those who need to know, for many parents the practical and emotional consequences of being so isolated are hard to bear. One mother told me how she was always worried about other people finding out and how she felt she had to make up complicated stories to explain why her child was not living at home. Even though she knew this was impossible, she felt like other people could see the truth simply by looking at her:

> *It feels like going round with a label on you. Like other people can see what's going on in your head and what's happened when you are walking down the street or shopping.* (Mother of a 12-year-old boy who had abused children in the neighbourhood)

Feelings of loss and grief

Finding out that your child has abused can be a hugely painful experience which can shatter your beliefs about yourself, your family and your child. It can be like something has died and gone forever:

> *It was like my child had died. Another child had been put in his place and I had to get to know the new one. I've grown to like the new one now, but the old one, my child, has gone forever.* (Mother of a 15-year-old young man who had abused his brother)

Like all situations where people experience loss, it is important that you are able to express your pain and grieve for what has been lost. Some of the pain here can be about thinking back to the past and seeing that there might have been clues or incidents which you saw as 'innocent' at the time, but that you now realise were problematic or abusive.

In support groups, parents who have been through this process have talked about how they never thought they would get through their feelings of grief, shock and disbelief. These feelings diminish with time and such parents provide inspiring and hopeful examples, showing that you can cope with life after the discovery of the abuse.

Confusion and uncertainty about sex

Often, one of the most difficult areas for parents to talk about is the effect of their child's sexually abusive behaviour on their own sex lives and relationships. Parents can experience uncertainty about sexual issues and feel that they no longer are able to enjoy sex. They can lose sight of what is normal and acceptable sexually, for themselves and for others.

Parents have talked about finding it hard to manage their feelings about abusers. It is also common to feel 'corrupted' by, or 'dirty' as a result of the details of the abuse, like you are seeing sexual abuse everywhere and in everyone, questioning people and situations you have thought innocent and OK previously. It can also be difficult for parents to see how their child could and should develop healthy sexual relationships in the future.

Feeling totally overwhelmed

Another of the most striking things for me in listening to parents talk about their experiences is the enormous weight placed on their shoulders by the abuse and how overwhelming this can be. There may be so many competing demands on your time and energies. This includes the burden of watching out for any examples of inappropriate behaviours, thinking about the abuse all the time, feeling uncertain about how best to act and not knowing where to turn for help.

Feeling out of control and powerless especially with professionals

Parents can feel powerless and out of control when faced with the involvement of professionals in their lives. Some parents have commented that they thought professionals held them in suspicion and did not recognise their need for support, and that they were the last to hear about decisions. Some mothers feel that professionals have relied heavily on them for the protection and care of other children and this can contribute to fathers' feeling that they are viewed as suspected perpetrators or unimportant in families.

Summary points from this section

- There is no one way you should feel as a parent whose child has sexually abused, but it is common and natural to feel overwhelmed and to struggle to cope.
- Parents often feel a mixture of shock, anger, denial, confusion, guilt, isolation and helplessness.
- Although you may never meet other parents in your position, you should remember that other parents in your position are experiencing similar feelings.
- Sharing the demands of the situation with a partner can relieve some of the pressure.
- You can be very isolated as a result of the abuse and having someone to support you and be aware that you may be feeling down can help.

Questions to consider

- How are you coping with the crisis of the sexual abuse?
- Who can support you?
- What can you do to get through the difficult times?
- How can you share the responsibilities fairly with your partner?

Tips for Dealing with the Situation

Get an accurate picture of what happened

You should find out the basic details of what has happened. This may be very painful but is likely to help in the longer-term. Some parents do not have an accurate picture of what has happened. This may be because professionals assume that parents have more knowledge than they have or because they use professional language that is not very clear for parents. Parents may have been scared to ask about the details. In these cases, parents can develop all kinds of ideas about what might have happened. Sometimes, parents fear the worse but when they find out about what has really happened they experience an enormous relief. Other times, their worst fears are confirmed. However, finding out the details of what happened is important as it allows you to know what you are dealing with. Professionals should be able to give you this information; you should not make any demands of a victim for information. The young person who has abused may need time to be able to give you an accurate picture:

> Sandra's fourteen-year-old son was due to go back to live with her, after staying in a children's home for 18 months following the abuse of his half-brother. Sandra was offered some sessions with her social worker to discuss how she could make her family situation safe. For the first time she asked and found out the details of what had happened. She explained how she had been having nightmares about what she imagined might have taken place. She commented that, had she known what had really gone on, she would have been able to help both her children with much more confidence earlier.

Sort out issues of responsibility and blame

Responsibility is an important concept in work with young people who have abused, and being able to think clearly about responsibility is a key challenge for parents. It is natural for parents to ask themselves whose fault the abuse is. Many parents feel that they must be to blame. It is not uncommon for parents to go back over the past with a fine tooth comb, reviewing all the ways in which they have influenced their child's behaviour and taking on all the blame for the abuse. Other parents find it hard to face up to the fact that their child has behaved in a sexually abusive way and think that the victim must share responsibility for what has happened or that the victim was not a victim at all but a willing participant in the sexual acts.

Many factors are likely to have contributed to your child's abusive behaviour, for some of which you may feel some responsibility. You may look back and wish that you had done some things differently. However, the one essential message to stress about responsibility for sexual abuse is that it is the abuser who is always responsible for the abuse, not the victim or the abuser's family. This holds as true for young people as it does for adults. For example, few would argue that an adult man who sexually abuses a four-year-old child is anything but 100 per cent responsible for the abuse. Asking your child to face up to his responsibility for the abuse does not mean 'blaming' him. Children and young people who have been damaged through being sexually abused themselves can go on to repeat their own experiences with other children. Despite their own experiences, it is important that these young people see that they are responsible for their own actions and that they have *chosen* to behave in an abusive way. Of course, it is important for us as adults to recognise why children made the poor choices they did and to support them in not making these choices again. However, defending children by claiming that it was not their fault may be a poor way of helping and may stop them from facing up to what they have done:

Sam was a seventeen-year-old young man who was accused of raping a fourteen-year-old young woman. His parents were so shocked that Sam had behaved this way they assumed that the victim must have been responsible for the sexual behaviour between the two young people. Sam had initially said that he was guilty, but his parents' views meant that it was easy for him to pretend to himself and others that he had been wrong to admit. He changed his statement and two years later was still maintaining his innocence.

Deal with denial

It is common for young people to deny that they have abused when they are accused or caught. In over ten years of working with children and young people who have sexually abused, I do not think I have ever met a young person who has been able to be honest about all of what he had done at the time that the abuse was discovered. You should not expect your child to tell you or anyone else the full story at first. This does not mean that you do not trust your child or that you are cynical. You are being realistic. Nobody enjoys being confronted with having done something wrong. Denial is an automatic reaction when we feel threatened. It is not surprising that children and young people, when faced with allegations as serious as sexual abuse, so frequently deny that anything has happened. Ultimately, this denial may not be in the best interest of your child if it stops him from facing up to the seriousness of his behaviour. Sometimes getting away with something by denying it at first means that it is harder to speak the truth later, as you not only have to face the truth of what you have done, but you have the added worry of having to admit that you lied about it as well.

Denial takes many forms. Some young people deny that they were there at the time of the abuse or deny that anything sexual has happened at all with the victim. In other situations, a young person may admit that something sexual happened but deny that it was abusive in any way. This may represent an attempt to make out that the victim was responsible or that there was no force involved. It is important for professionals and parents together to give a young person as many opportunities as possible to face up to what he has done. Some young people hold on to some denial even when they begin to admit some aspects of the truth. For example, a young person might admit to touching a child, but deny penetrating her. Provided that the young person can admit to something having happened, this gives a platform for the therapy or treatment work to take place.

Young people can also be very skilled in their denial. It can be extremely difficult as a parent to see through your child's denial. Often there is little for you as a parent to go on except what your child is saying, as you have so little information about what the victim has said. Here are some tips for dealing with your child's denial:

- Keep an open mind about what your child tells you.
- Don't 'rubbish' or humiliate your child by confronting him in an angry or sarcastic way.
- Practise making statements which allow your child to climb down at some point without feeling doubly bad. Say things that allow the possibility of admission later, for example, 'I am pleased you have been able to tell me as much as you have. If there are other things you need to let me know of in the future, that's fine' or if the child is denying anything happened 'I know you are telling me nothing happened at all, but if you remember that something else happened, you can always tell me. I would be proud of you for facing up to the truth', etc.

- Get as much information as you can from other sources about what is alleged to have happened so that you minimise the possibility of being fed a series of untruths by your child. Obviously, you need to get this information through appropriate channels, such as a professional. For example, in a planning meeting Sheila asked some direct questions about what her son, Jamie, had been able to say in his treatment. Sheila realised for the first time that Jamie had given her a totally different account at home. If professionals do not offer the information you need, seek it out and ask them directly.

- Concentrate on what the young person is prepared to admit to, rather than calling him a liar, e.g. 'it's good that we both agree that what happened with Gemma was wrong, even though you feel that it hasn't hurt her at all'.

Confronting your own denial

It is not only young people who can respond with denial. Parents, and indeed professionals, can also fall into this trap. As a parent, you may feel so shocked or horrified about an allegation made against your child that you want to deny the truth, either to yourself or to other people. Try to keep an open mind about what has happened. Even if you are unsure as to how serious the behaviour is, try to understand why other people might be worried. Think about the evidence available to you. Children hardly ever make up allegations of sexual abuse. Indeed, they usually hide or downplay it rather than make it up or exaggerate it. If you are not sure about something, say so. You do not always have to be sure or definite about things. For example, it is fine to say to professionals 'I know that you believe this to be true, but I am struggling to believe or understand this and I need some more time and some help to face this.'

Summary points from this section

- Getting basic information about what happened from a professional can be useful in helping your child to recover and in making your situation safe. Without this information, you don't know what you are dealing with.

- Victims are never to blame for the abuse. Young people who have sexually abused need to be helped to take responsibility for their actions.

- Almost all young people deny or minimise their behaviours in some way, especially when the abuse has just been discovered.

- You can help your child by responding to denial in a way which will allow your child to face up to their behaviours.

Questions to consider

- What do you already know about what happened and where are the gaps in your knowledge?

- How can you encourage your child to take appropriate responsibility?

- Can you practise ways of responding to your child's denial, both in what you say and what you do?

Exercise 5: Sorting out what you do and don't know and getting the information you need

Purpose. This exercise is designed to help you to look more closely at what you know already about the abuse and to identify other information that could help you.

1. Use the boxes below to figure out what you know for sure about your child's abuse, what you are unsure about and what you definitely need to find out more about.

What I know definitely happened:

What I suspect happened but am not sure about:

What I don't yet know and need to find out:

2. In the left hand column, write down a list of specific questions to ask to get the information you need. Then think about who can give you the information and how best you might approach this person. Bear in mind the different status of the people concerned and therefore the different approaches you need to take. For example, if you needed to ask your child something, you would need to think carefully about what words to use, how best to approach him, the right time and place, etc. Remember that it is not appropriate to make demands on victims for information about what happened. If in any doubt about whether to approach someone for information and how to do this, seek advice from a professional.

Specific questions to help me get the information I need:	The most appropriate person to give me the information is:	How I can get the information from this person (e.g. best way to approach the subject, best time and place):

Exercise 6: Responsibility: sorting out feelings of guilt, shame and blame

Purpose. This information will help you to look at issues of responsibility and to separate out what you are, and are not, responsible for.

Feelings of guilt can often block people from taking the steps required to face up to abuse. Feelings of shame can be particularly destructive. Both of these feelings, whilst they can be the emotional consequence of facing up to the truth, are different from facing responsibility. In facing responsibility you are taking steps towards untangling the mess that sexual abuse can create in your family. Sorting out responsibility issues lays a foundation for you and other people to change the bigger picture. It is also about fairness: making sure that nobody is left feeling to blame or holding responsibility for things that were not their fault.

1. Things that make you feel guilty and ashamed:

In the left-hand column, make a list of all the reasons you feel guilty or ashamed following your child's abuse. These can be as logical or illogical, or big or small as you like.

   In the right hand column write down messages you can give yourself in response to the things you have written on the left. These may be corrections to feelings of guilt or shame, e.g. 'You should not feel guilty for this because...' or they may be messages of hope for the future.

I feel guilty because:	Corrections/messages:
I feel ashamed because:	

2. Looking at responsibility

Use the four boxes below to separate out what you and your child are and are not responsible for.

Things I **am** responsible for as the parent of my child	Things that my child (who has abused) **is** responsible for
Things I am **not** responsible for as the parent of my child	Things that my child is **not** responsible for:

Now look again at the things you have written. If you are to 'make it fair' following the abuse, is there anyone else who might need to accept some responsibility?

....

....

3. Ways of facing responsibility

3.1 What I need to do to face up to the things I am responsible for:

....

....

3.2 What my child needs to do to face up to the things he is responsible for:

....

....

3.3 Ways I can help my child take on this responsibility:

....

....

Exercise 7: Giving voice to your feelings

Purpose. This exercise is designed to help you to examine and express your feelings in an appropriate way.

Many parents whose children have sexually abused would like to say things to their child, but cannot because this process is too scary or inappropriate. Writing things down in a letter which **is not sent** can be one way of working out your feelings and giving a voice to all the things you are struggling to cope with inside. You can voice all your feelings without worrying about how the other person would feel.

Writing a Letter

1. Write a letter addressed to your child (not to be sent) which includes the following points:
   - What it was about the things that happened that were not OK, that caused you pain and hurt.
   - What feelings you have been left with as a result of the abuse.
   - What you think of your child now.
   - What you understand now about why your child acted in this way.
   - What is different about your life as a result of the abuse.
   - Any other things that you would like to say to your child or questions to which you have not yet found an answer.

   It is best to write quickly and not to stop thoughts that come into your head by thinking too hard. Let the ideas flow.

2. After you have written the letter, go through it and underline any messages or points you think would be important, appropriate and safe to say in reality to your child. Discuss these with your partner, professional, etc. to decide on whether, when and how to say these things.

Alternatives

3. Writing down thoughts and feelings in the form of a letter which is not sent can be used in a number of ways. If your have found this exercise to be helpful, you can try the following alternative versions:
   - A letter to yourself. Here you can give yourself messages about what you need to do to cope with your feelings, or to make changes to your life, etc.
   - A letter to the victim of your child's abuse, explaining your feelings to them. Here you can talk about your feelings about the victim's experience. Again, this letter **must not be sent**, but setting out your feelings in this way can help.
   - A letter to the your child when he is an adult. Here you can address all the things you hope for your child in the future and how you wish him to progress.

Exercise 8: A plan for dealing with the pain

Purpose. This exercise encourages you to look back at the particular aspects of your situation that cause you pain and to think about what you can do to lessen this pain.

Like physical pain, you cannot simply take emotional pain away, but there are things you can do to cope with it and, in some cases, to reduce the level of the pain. Some of the ways that people cope with pain are healthy and appropriate, others may be unhealthy, inappropriate and have damaging side-effects. For example, parents who drink too much alcohol may be damaging their health and may make them less able to cope with other life situations and less able to manage risk.

1. Make a list of the five most painful things about your situation:

1.1

1.2

1.3

1.4

1.5

2. What effect the pain is having on you:

....

....

3. Healthy things you can do to help reduce or 'massage' the pain:

....

....

4. Negative ways to reduce the pain which you should avoid and why:

....

....

5. Try to draw up some specific goals or activities that will help you to cope with or 'massage' the pain. List the five most helpful points in order of importance:

5.1

5.2

5.3

5.4

5.5

What If the Victim is Also Your Child?

If you are a parent of a young person who has sexually abused another of your children, you deserve a special mention here. This is sometimes referred to as 'sibling sexual abuse'. Parents in these situations face a difficult task as they have to cope with the needs of both children. Sometimes loyalties are stretched to breaking point. You want the best for the child who has abused, but how do you balance this with supporting the child who has been victimised? You may also feel extremely guilty, like Anne, a mother of a 13-year-old young man who had abused his sister:

> *To think that it was going on in my house, under my nose, without me seeing it. It makes me feel sick. Why didn't I see what was going on? Why couldn't she tell me? I thought I was so close to my kids, I thought I'd brought them up to love each other. I always told them to come to me if they had a problem.*

There may be many reasons why you did not see what was happening in your family and why a child who was close to you could not tell you about the abuse at the time, including:

- The child who was victimised may have believed that the abuse was what happens normally with brothers or sisters in all families.
- The child being abused might have worried about your feelings were you to find out. She might have thought you would be upset.
- The victim might have thought that she would not have been believed if she had told.
- The victim might have been made to feel by the brother or sister doing the abusing that she was partly responsible and that you would be angry with them both.

Sibling sexual abuse often raises dilemmas about divided loyalties for victims. Victims will often want the abuse to stop, but still care for the brother or sister who is abusing them. Because they know that the sibling abusing them would get into trouble if they were to tell someone about the abuse, they 'sacrifice' themselves and decide to put up with the behaviours to protect the brother or sister. Sibling sexual abuse can also be very complex and can involve more than two children. Other victims can be brought into the situation in different ways, as in the following case examples:

> **Example One:** Brian (aged fifteen) abused his younger brother, Mark (aged eight) and Dominic (aged six). Sometimes, Brian would force Mark and Dominic to do sexual things together when he watched. Mark became 'sexualised', i.e. he began seeing things and people in a very sexual way, and started to abuse Dominic himself even when Brian was not around.

> **Example Two:** George, aged twelve at the time, had been sexually abused by his male cousin and his mother. He had four brothers, younger and older than him, all of whom had been abused by the same cousin. All of the brothers started to do sexual things with each other in the family home.

> **Example Three:** Sarah (aged six) was abused by Alan (aged fifteen) for several years. She began to expect sexual abuse from all males. Later her other brother, Sean (aged thirteen) started to do sexual things to her too. But Alan and Sean did not do sexual things with each other and did not know of each other's abuse of Sarah.

These three examples show just how complicated situations of sibling sexual abuse can be and how sexual abuse can sometimes become an integral part of how siblings behave towards each other in families.

As parents, facing up to sibling sexual abuse can be particularly painful. You cannot wind back the clock, but it is possible and necessary to look seriously at changing the way that your family has operated and altering the environment in your family in order to protect all children who have been, or may be, affected by the abuse. This involves making it safe for all children in the family. Even those who may not have been directly sexually abused may have been affected by the undertones or the 'dynamics' associated with the abuse. It is also important to see the abuse for what it is, rather than giving in to the temptation of thinking that the behaviours were just natural experimentation between brothers and sisters. We know from the accounts of abuse survivors that sexual abuse is not any less serious or painful just because the victim and abuser are related. In fact, sibling abuse is likely to have gone on for longer before being discovered, involved more incidents of abuse and is very painful for victims.

Sometimes, the dynamics of sibling sexual abuse mean that parents can struggle to see whether they should treat their child as a 'victim' or 'abuser' especially in situations like that of Mark in Example One above. The important thing in such situations is to see your child as an individual with needs and problems, rather than getting confused or tied up with how to describe them. Both parts of Mark's experience, what was done to him by Brian *and* what he did to Dominic, need to be taken into account and addressed in any therapy with him. Neither is more significant or important than the other and Mark would probably struggle to make sense of one side of his experience without the other. The most important thing is to make it safe for all concerned and to stop all aspects of the abuse.

Summary points from this section

- Sibling sexual abuse often makes it very difficult for parents to balance the different needs of their children.
- It can be a complex issue and involve more than just two children.
- Victims of sibling sexual abuse may well want to protect the sibling who has abused them.

Questions to consider

- If one of your children has abused another, what can you do to meet all your children's needs?
- Are you acknowledging the seriousness of the behaviours?
- Do you need to put any more measures in place in order to protect all the children in your family?

Chapter 3
Why has this Happened?

About the Search for 'Why'

For many parents, the need to search for reasons for the abuse is a long-term struggle. Having accepted that the abuse has taken place, most parents are uncertain about why their child has behaved in this way and what this means about them. Typical questions can include 'does this mean he is a paedophile' or 'does this mean he is gay?' In order to help your child, it is important to develop some ideas about what might have influenced your child's behaviour, to understand the motivation behind the abuse and to think about what it might mean for the future. Parents often want to know 'why' because they are anxious that their child has abused as a result of something they have done, or have failed to do, as parents. One message is not to take up so much time trying to figure out 'why' that you do not get round to doing some of the other important things you can do to help, such as making your family situation safe or supporting your child in any treatment work. Keep an open mind on why your child may have behaved in a sexually abusive way and do not jump to conclusions which could be over-simplistic or wrong.

This chapter explores in more detail the possible reasons 'why' young people abuse. However, you should bear the following two points in mind:

1. You may not find a simple answer

You may never find out exactly why your child abused. Often professionals will only be able to say that certain things may have come together to influence your child's behaviour. It can be unhelpful to think that one single thing is the key to the question 'why?' For example, think back to something you did at some point in your life that you later regretted very much. Ask yourself why you did it. You might see that you were influenced in a whole range of ways by your experiences, your feelings at the time and the example of other people around you. Having to find the one single thing that made you behave in this way might be oversimplifying what was a complex process. You might also realise that, despite all the influences on you, you were still responsible for what you chose to do.

2. Your child probably does not know why

I find that most young people who sexually abuse genuinely have little or no real awareness of why they have behaved in this way, especially in the early stages of my work with them. When asked this question they often simply say 'I don't know' or 'it just happened'. Using the same example you chose above, think about how aware you were at the time of why you did what you did? What would you have said at the time if someone had asked you to explain 'why'? You might have felt ashamed or guilty or angry, but probably you would have not been able to give an accurate answer to this. Maybe you still cannot?

Pathways into Sexually Abusive Behaviour

Much of the work done with young people who have sexually abused is designed to try to help them think and learn about the thoughts, feelings and life experiences which may have come together to influence their behaviour. Young people often find it useful to think of this as their 'pathway' into abusive behaviour.

In order to understand what this means, think of yourself undertaking a long journey somewhere by car. There are many possible routes you could take. Some may be direct, others more winding. When you are underway, there may be things that happen that make you stop altogether (e.g. traffic lights, accidents), change direction (e.g. a blocked road) or go slowly (e.g. traffic jam). At other points you will speed ahead and go quickly in the right direction. At any point you could decide to turn around and go back home, or go somewhere else instead.

Similarly, a young person's pathway into sexually abusive behaviour may not be straightforward. A pathway to abuse involves lots of 'steps' which take the young person nearer to behaving in an abusive way. These steps can be influenced by many different things; experiences a child has had which have sent the child in a particular direction, emotional difficulties or problems, things that might happen more by chance. Each forward step towards the abusive behaviour brings the young person closer to abusing. Other experiences might divert a young person away from the abusive behaviour (e.g. having a caring parent), but if the steps a young person takes **towards** abuse are stronger than the steps **away** from it, the young person may abuse.

Common experiences which can 'lead' a young person in the direction of sexually abusive behaviour

Whilst each young person's pathway towards abusive behaviour is in some way unique, there are some influences that are often commonly found to have pushed young people forward in the direction of abuse. On their own they do not explain why a child has abused. There are many children who have these life experiences who do not go on to abuse, but for those who do abuse, the following range of experiences may have been significant:

- **Experiencing sexual abuse.** Having a past history of sexual abuse may lead a young person to learn incorrect messages about sex, to think about sex in situations which are not sexual and to want to try out sexual things on others in the same way in which they were abused. For example, Amy was sixteen but had been the victim of sexual abuse all though her childhood from her step-father. She thought that all she was good for was sex and she saw sex in all her relationships even when the other person did not. In the children's home where Amy lived, she put pressure on a twelve-year-old boy to have sex with her against his will.

- **Experiencing physical abuse.** Being physically abused can lead children to have a low opinion of themselves, which in turn can stop them developing healthy sexual relationships. The experience of being physically abused may make a child believe that using physical and sexual violence and force is an acceptable way of behaving towards another person. Sajid was a fifteen-year-old young man who had been severely physically abused in his childhood. He felt lonely and bitter in the children's home he lived in and he bullied other children there, sometimes in a sexual way.

- **Being subjected to sexual imagery or pornography.** Children and young people can become 'corrupted' and influenced by sexual images and pornography, particularly if other experiences or relationships in their lives are difficult or problematic. Michael spent hours on the Internet and became obsessed with looking at pictures of hardcore pornography. He had no girlfriend or opportunity to explore the things he was seeing which made him sexually aroused. He abused his sister.

- **Lack of accurate sexual knowledge.** Not knowing enough about sex can make it difficult for young people to make the right kind of decisions about sex and to cope with the overwhelming sexual feelings that can come with being a teenager. Stuart had a learning disability and had not received any sex education. His body started to develop sexually and he was confused by his strong sexual thoughts. He had no understanding of acceptable and unacceptable sexual behaviours. He also had few friends and started to follow women in the street and assaulted them by touching their breasts and running off.

- **Being given too much responsibility.** Having caring responsibilities towards younger children in the family may give a young person access to children, put him in a powerful position over the children, and at the same time stop the young person having relationships outside of the family. For example, Andrew (aged fifteen) was given all responsibility for the care of his two younger sisters and younger brother. He would get them up in the morning, give them their breakfast and get them ready for school. In the evening he would bath them and prepare them for bed. He began to view the children as his closest emotional supports and felt most at ease when he was with them. When he started to do sexual things to them, the children were so dependent upon him that they did not question what Andrew was doing to them.

- **Feeling left out and lonely.** Feeling lonely and isolated amongst people of the same age and feeling left out sexually is a common experience for young people who sexually abuse. Mark was a lonely fourteen-year-old, who looked younger than others in his class. He was laughed at by his classmates and teased because of a minor facial disfigurement. He felt comfortable only when he was with younger children and spent hours playing with an eight-year-old neighbour, whom he saw as his girlfriend and later abused.

- **Feeling different or bad about yourself.** This can be the case especially if such feelings are connected to sexual things or sexuality. Darren, aged fourteen, was an isolated young man who was gay. The messages he received from his family were that gay people were evil and dirty and should not be tolerated. Darren began to believe that this applied to him. He felt guilt about his sexual thoughts and yet desperately wanted to try out sex. He abused his younger male cousin.

It may be easy to see how some of these experiences might lead a young person strongly down a pathway of sexually abusive behaviour. An example of this is a young person's own past history of sexual abuse. However, other experiences, such as feeling lonely or isolated, or feeling bad about oneself, are clearly common experiences for many children and young people at some points in their lives. The important point about all of these factors or experiences is that it is the **build-up** of these kinds of negative thoughts, feelings and experiences that can damage a child's sense of identity and can lead a child in the direction of sexual problems. So, a one-off experience of isolation is not likely to set a child off on a pathway of abusive behaviour. But as the pile of difficulties and problems begin to mount up for a child, the more likely it is that he will develop negative or problematic behaviours, some of them possibly sexual in nature. A child who has been sexually abused, *and* physically abused, *and* given too much responsibility for looking after children, *and* who is lonely and isolated from people of his own age is more likely to travel on a pathway of abusive behaviour than a child who has had only one of these experiences. Like an actual journey, large distances towards sexually abusive behaviour can be travelled by taking relatively small steps.

Stages in the development of sexually abusive behaviours

As well as the 'steps' leading a young person in the direction of sexually abusive behaviour, we can also envisage the overall pathway as involving a number of distinct **stages**. Each of these stages is made up of steps, and may be described as 'preconditions' (Finkelhor, 1984). In other words, they are the conditions that need to be present for a person to abuse. This demonstrates how sexually abusive behaviour does not just happen spontaneously, but has a number of different elements to it. If we can understand what these different elements or stages are for any given young person, that young person can be guided back onto non-abusive pathways.

The following diagram shows the common stages which can make up a young person's pathway to abusive behaviour:

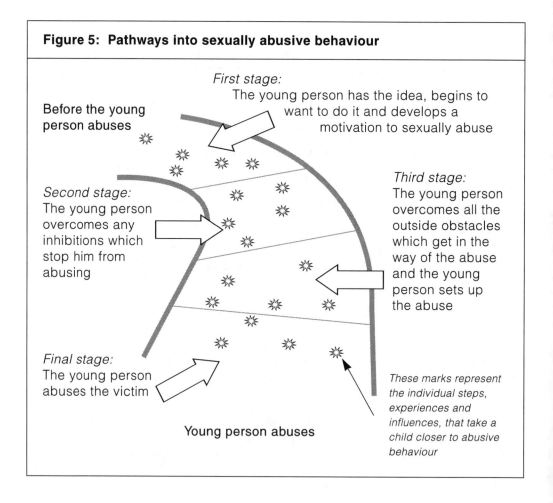

Figure 5: Pathways into sexually abusive behaviour

Before the young person abuses

First stage:
The young person has the idea, begins to want to do it and develops a motivation to sexually abuse

Second stage:
The young person overcomes any inhibitions which stop him from abusing

Third stage:
The young person overcomes all the outside obstacles which get in the way of the abuse and the young person sets up the abuse

Final stage:
The young person abuses the victim

Young person abuses

These marks represent the individual steps, experiences and influences, that take a child closer to abusive behaviour

Each of the stages is described in more detail below:

Stage one: having a motivation to abuse

According to this way of looking at sexual abuse, the first step on the pathway to sexually abusive behaviour is to have a 'motivation' to sexually abuse. Motivation in this sense refers to the factors in young people's lives which **encourage** them, **urge** them or **make them want to** sexually abuse.

Young people can be 'motivated' to sexually abuse as a result of their past experiences which might have left them feeling worthless, damaged or hurt in some way. For some young people this may include experiences of sexual abuse which have planted the seed of sexually abusive behaviour in their thoughts. Some young people's motivation to act sexually with younger children comes from the fact that they have come to identify emotionally with younger children rather than young people their own age and they start to find younger children sexually attractive. For other young people, younger children are an outlet for their sexual frustrations given their sense of being isolated from their peers.

Andrew was a thirteen-year-old who sexually abused his brother, Alex. Andrew had been sexually abused himself when he was a small boy. He had experienced the loss of his father who left the family when he was twelve and recently his grandmother, to whom he was close, had died. Andrew was lonely and isolated, with no friends. He felt left out when other children talked of their sexual experiences. He had recently entered into puberty and had many sexual urges that made him confused following his own abuse. All of these things seemed to come together for Andrew to give him a 'motivation' to abuse.

Stage two: overcoming internal inhibitions

Simply having a motivation to abuse does not mean that the person concerned will go as far as carrying out abuse. Many people experience urges sometimes to do something which is deviant or wrong (not necessarily sexual) but never actually act on their urges. It may be that common sense or an awareness of the consequences helps them conquer the urge and keep their self-control. Similarly, for a young person to sexually abuse he has to overcome any inhibitions or internal 'messages' that say that sexual abuse is wrong and that the young person should not do it. In other words, this second stage is one where the young person tries to convince himself that it would be OK to act on abusive thoughts. In order to break down these inhibitions (or become 'dis-inhibited') young people may develop incorrect or distorted beliefs, attitudes and thoughts which support the idea of sexually abusive behaviour. These are commonly referred to as 'cognitive distortions' or 'thinking errors' by professionals. Examples of these are:

- 'It wouldn't do any harm'.
- 'It's OK for adolescents to have sex with small children'.
- 'Children need adolescents to teach them about sex so that they don't get hurt'.

Sometimes young people have managed to convince themselves that these thinking errors are true, other times a young person's life experiences reinforce these distortions. Mostly though, young people know all too well that abuse is wrong. In such situations, young people may use drugs or alcohol to get over their inhibitions. In other words, they may feel freer to behave in abusive ways when they have used drugs or drink. Alternatively, certain mood states (for instance when feeling very depressed, lonely or angry) may lead them to give more weight in their heads to the distorted or faulty thinking. Andrew told me that this was like:

> *...having a 'devil' on one shoulder telling him to go ahead and abuse, and an 'angel' on his other shoulder saying that it was wrong. Some days, he said, he listened to the angel, but increasingly as time went by, the 'devil's' argument was the strongest.*

Stage three: getting over all the outside obstacles

The first two stages examined above are 'internal' to a young person. The third stage on the pathway to abuse is for the young person to get over all the outside (or external) obstacles to abusing. Put simply, a young person might have a motivation to abuse and might have no inhibitions which stop him, but still have no opportunities to act on the thoughts. Obstacles might include:

- never being alone with a child
- being watched closely
- the way that a family is organised.

The third stage, then, is for a young person to create opportunities to abuse. This often involves thinking through or fantasising about abusing a child and trying to win the child's and other people's trust in order to prepare the child (or other people who might otherwise protect her) for sexual abuse in the future. This process is often called the 'grooming process' by professionals and refers to the effort that young people can put into slowly moving towards sexual abuse. For example Andrew spent many hours alone with Alex playing hide-and-seek in his bedroom away from adult supervision. He did this deliberately as this helped him to create situations when he could introduce more and more touch and physical contact into their play.

Stage four: doing it

The final stage is committing the abuse itself which requires forcing the victim into the sexual act, taking measures not to get caught and trying to make it less likely that the victim will speak out about the abuse, or be believed.

Andrew thought about acting upon his sexual thoughts and abusing his brother for several weeks, until one day his mother left them alone in the house whilst she went to call on a neighbour. Andrew had been imagining this for some time, planning and becoming sexually aroused to thoughts of what he could do were he to find himself in such a situation with Alex. He asked his brother if he wanted to play hide and seek. Of course Alex was very keen to do this as Andrew had built up this as a game for so long. This time, Andrew made sure the front door was locked, the curtains were closed and nobody could see into his bedroom where he hid under the covers. When Alex came to find him, Andrew sexually assaulted him. Afterwards he warned Alex not to tell their mother about the 'game' they had played. He carefully went downstairs to unlock the door and make it seem as if nothing had happened.

Patterns of Sexually Abusive Behaviour

Once young people, like Andrew above, have gone down the pathway of sexually abusive behaviour, it can be very hard for them to get off it or to move back to a non-abusive path. Professionals working with young people often see young people who have become trapped in patterns of sexually abusive behaviour over time. This can almost be like an addiction. To help explain why a young person can be trapped in patterns of behaviour, many professionals use the idea of a 'cycle' of sexually abusive behaviour (Ryan and Lane, 1991).

Being trapped in a pattern or cycle of behaviour is not unique to sexual abuse however. Many kinds of unhealthy behaviours tend to follow patterns. In other words, they do not just happen once but tend to occur again and again over a period of time. The behaviours do not just appear 'out of the blue', but are connected to patterns of feelings and thoughts. Here are two everyday examples of cycles of negative behaviour:

1. **Dorothy** loves chocolate. She is overweight and is on a diet, which she manages to stick to most of the time. Sometimes though she gets bored at home and starts to feel down. She thinks 'what's the point of dieting when no-one pays any attention to me or the way I look anyway'. She begins to think about eating the large bar of chocolate that she knows is hidden away at the back of her cupboard. She tries to justify this by saying to herself that she'll only eat one piece and that won't harm her diet. She takes out the chocolate and eats her one piece. It tastes so good that she has another piece. She thinks 'what the hell' and very soon she has eaten the whole bar. Afterwards she feels that she has ruined all her efforts to diet and feels like a real loser. She says to herself that this is the last time and that she definitely won't eat any more chocolate.

2. **Dennis** can't stop buying lottery scratchcards. He has promised his wife that he won't do this as the amount he is spending on scratchcards is leaving the family without enough money for food. At first he manages not to buy any. But one night on his way home from work he passes a newsagents. He persuades himself that he should go in to buy a newspaper, but really he is fooling himself and once he is inside he can't resist buying a scratchcard...or two, or three. Afterwards he feels like he has let himself down, but he acts as if nothing has happened. He promises himself he won't do it again.

Can you:

- Be confident that Dorothy and Dennis will keep their promises to themselves and not repeat the behaviours?
- Identify how the two people's feelings influenced their actions?
- Identify how the two people changed their thoughts, or tried to convince themselves, that their actions were OK even when they knew they were not?

Both Dennis and Dorothy are caught in negative patterns of behaviour that make them do the things that they have promised to themselves and others that they would not. They are both 'addicted' to the behaviours and to the feelings that the behaviours give them. Although they tell themselves that it will not happen again, left to themselves, they are unlikely to be able to stop the behaviour.

It may seem strange that I have offered two examples of fairly ordinary behaviours that most people on some level might be able to identify with. I do not, of course, wish to suggest that sexually abusive behaviour is ordinary, but there are some things we can learn from the examples above to help understand why a young person might get trapped in a pattern of sexually abusive behaviour. In similar but more serious ways, young people can become 'addicted' to the feelings they experience when they sexually abuse someone. Although the idea of the cycle of abuse **does not explain what causes** a child to abuse in the first place, it can help to describe how the behaviours can become fixed within a continuous pattern. The cycle can be represented as follows:

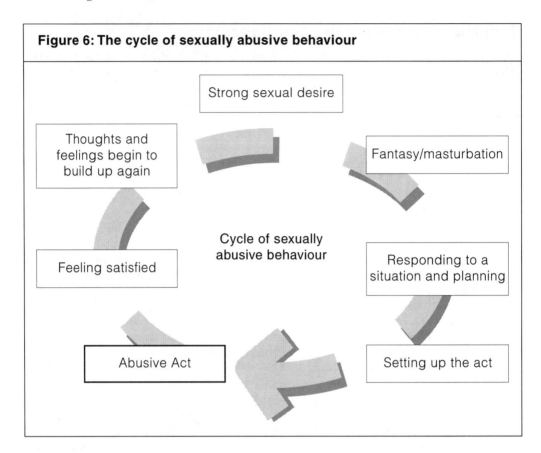

Figure 6: The cycle of sexually abusive behaviour

Strong sexual desire

Thoughts and feelings begin to build up again

Fantasy/masturbation

Cycle of sexually abusive behaviour

Feeling satisfied

Responding to a situation and planning

Abusive Act

Setting up the act

The idea of the cycle can be described as follows:

The young person experiences a **strong sexual desire** or an urge to act in a sexual way. This sexual urge may be triggered by an event or situation which leaves the young person with a feeling he cannot cope with. The young person may start to think about sex (or sexual abuse) as a way of trying to make himself feel better. The young person may masturbate to **thoughts or fantasies** of sex or abuse. The sexual feelings this leads to can block off any messages telling the young person not to abuse and can reinforce 'distorted' thoughts about the abuse being OK, not harmful or simply a 'good idea'. The young person then puts himself in a **situation** where he can act on the fantasy which has been going around in his head. Sometimes this is **planned** in advance and carefully set up. Other times, the young person **takes advantage of a situation** he suddenly finds himself in. Once in a situation where abuse is possible, a young person **abuses**. Many young people say that they gain an **intense feeling of sexual excitement** leading up to the abuse and **sexual satisfaction** during the abuse. After having abused, a young person may often feel **sexually relieved or calmer**. There may also be some **feelings of regret or worry** about what he has done, but which the young person may try not to think about or dwell upon. There may be a period of time when the young person tells himself that he won't abuse again, but when the **sexual feelings start to build up again**, these messages become weakened and the cycle may then begin again.

The whole process may be very quick. For some young people, it can start to happen each time they see a child. For others, it takes a significant amount of time to go round this cycle once. Returning to the example of Andrew demonstrates how this pattern or cycle of behaviour can become fixed and increasingly addictive:

> Once Andrew had abused Alex the first time, he felt a short period of sexual satisfaction, but this did not last for long. He began to think about what else he could do to Alex, what other things he could try out. He became aroused thinking about this over a period of two days and masturbated to pictures in his head of him doing what he did the last time but this time going further. He thought that he should not do it again, because he knew it was wrong, but at the same time, Alex had not said anything to their mother and Andrew began to tell himself that Alex must have thought it was a good game and must have enjoyed it. After two days of thinking about doing it again, Andrew started another game of hide and seek upstairs, this time whilst his mother was downstairs. He abused Alex again. As time went on, the abuse became a regular thing that Andrew did to Alex.

Here are the words Andrew used to try to describe the pattern of behaviour he became trapped in. I have changed them only slightly to help the meaning become clearer. Andrew wrote this account whilst he was in a therapy group in which he had learnt about cycles of behaviour:

> *On the outside everything seemed normal. I was curious about sex and felt that I should someway find out about it. I had it on my mind as people were tormenting me and asking me questions (about sex) that I didn't know. My mum was giving me a hard time at home and then my kind of best friend died: my gran the following month. Because my mum was worked up about gran's death, sometimes she took it out on me. I had problems in school and I was stressed and worried.*
>
> *At school kids started to get to me. They were all talking about sex they had had and I thought that I was missing out. More and more sexual things built up in me. Everything near enough reached the highest point until one day my brother came to my room and sat on my bed. A sudden idea came to me to touch him between the legs. I got an erection thinking about it, but I didn't do anything...But I couldn't stop thinking about it.*
>
> *The next time we were alone, when my mum was out of the house I mean, I asked him to play a game of hide and seek. I touched him on his penis and asked him to touch me on my penis...I did feel bad afterwards because I knew it was wrong to do this with your brother. I promised myself that it wouldn't happen again, but it felt good and I really wanted to get that feeling again.*
>
> *From then on, it happened every time there was a chance. I did other things too, became braver. It probably happened two or three times a week for about six months. In the end I only needed to look at him and he could tell what I wanted. Then one day, when I came home from school, my mum was standing there and I knew that she knew.*

Implications for your Child of Pathways and Patterns of Sexually Abusive Behaviour

The ideas of pathways and patterns of abuse can be helpful in trying to understand why your child may have abused. However, it is important to remember that these are just ways of trying to understand how a young person's sexually abusive behaviour can develop and be maintained. At the same time, it is important to see your child as an individual whose abusive behaviours and patterns of abuse may be different from those of Andrew or the other young people I discuss in this book. Understanding the *idea* of the cycle of abuse is important, as it is often used by projects who work with children and young people to teach them about sexually abusive behaviour. Your child may ask you questions about this or tell you that he has been doing work to identify his own cycle. Learning about pathways and patterns of sexually abusive behaviour may also raise particular questions for you as parents, such as:

Does the idea of a pathway mean that my child would not have sexually abused if it hadn't been for his own sexual abuse in the past?

The idea of 'pathways' into sexually abusive behaviour might have made you think about the influence of your own child's sexual abuse on his behaviour. Some parents struggle with trying to put this in its correct place, such as 'if my child hadn't been abused, he would not have gone on to abuse others'. Sexual abuse, or other forms of abuse, can be a really significant step for young people towards abusive behaviour. It may be true that your child would not have abused were it not for his own experiences of abuse, but there are many children who have been abused yet do not go on to abuse other people. Sexual abuse is usually only one step and it is important to work out what other things may have contributed.

Does the idea of a cycle of abuse mean that my child is going to grow up to be a paedophile and carry on abusing? Is there no way out of the cycle?

As we have seen, it is likely that many factors came together for your child to progress down his pathway towards abusive behaviour. Your child may also have become caught in a pattern or cycle of abuse over time. But the ideas of the pathway and cycle of abusive behaviour show that other events and choices could have diverted your child away from abuse. It is possible for the cycle to be broken and for your child to find an non-abusive pathway in the future. You may have read and been told that most adult sex offenders started to abuse in their childhood or adolescence. This may well leave you worried about your child's future. However, it is not automatic that a young person will go on to commit further sexual abuse as an adult. With help, support and monitoring you can give your child the best chance to be one of the majority of young people who, it is now believed, manage to break their cycle of abusive behaviour.

Summary points from this section

- Thinking about why a child sexually abuses is complex.
- You may never be able to find a simple answer to this question.
- Understanding what might have contributed to your child's behaviour can help you to identify what needs to change.
- The idea of pathways into sexually abusive behaviour shows how many different experiences and factors may have influenced your child.
- The idea of the cycle of sexually abusive behaviour demonstrates how a young person can become trapped in a repeating pattern of behaviour, as if the young person becomes 'addicted' to the feelings he gains from abusing.

Questions to consider

- Can you look back at your child's development and see any experiences that might have motivated or influenced your child to behave in this way?
- Can you identify any ways in which you could try to stop your child becoming trapped in a cycle of abusive behaviours?

Exercise 9:   Looking back at your child's developmental history

Purpose. This exercise is designed to help you look back at your child's life and to think about significant events. These might give you some clues as to the influences or steps involved in your child's pathway into abuse.

1. Using the lines provided as a guide, mark with a cross on the life line all the significant life events you recall in your child's development. In the space above the line, note each of these briefly. Include anything you feel is significant, e.g. births, deaths, changes, specific incidents.

2. Then take a different coloured pen. Using the lines provided, mark in the bottom part (below the line) all incidents of a sexual nature that you are aware your child has engaged in.

Child's general life history

0 yrs	2 yrs	4 yrs	6 yrs	8 yrs	10 yrs	12 yrs	14 yrs	16 yrs	18 yrs

Child's sexual life history

Exercise 10: Charting your child's pathway into abuse

Purpose. This exercise is designed to help you look at what might have been significant in your child's pathway into abusive behaviour.

Before my child was abusing

First stage
What might have set your child off on the first step of sexually abusive behaviour? What could your child's motivation have been?

....
....
....
....
....

Second stage
How might your child have persuaded himself that it was OK to abuse?

....
....
....
....
....

Third stage
What obstacles were in your child's way and how did your child get in a position to abuse?
Who did your child choose to abuse and why?

....
....
....
....
....

Fourth stage
What choices did your child make about when and how he abused and what he did to make it secret?

....
....
....
....
....

My child sexually abused

Chapter 4
Meeting your own Needs

It may seem strange that I have included a chapter on meeting your needs as parents at this point in this book. You may be inundated with demands to help your family and sort out practical issues. It may be that no one appears to have considered your needs. However, you should pay attention to yourself and your needs in order to be in a position to help your child. If you are in a relationship, this will need attention too.

Dealing with the Impact of your Child's Behaviour on you as an Individual

Trust and Forgiveness

For parents whose children have sexually abused, the question 'when should I trust my child again?' is often difficult. Some parents have said that they feel guilty because there are situations where they do not 'trust' the young person who has abused. They wonder whether this is unfair or somehow makes them bad or unnatural as parents. Certainly, you should not feel guilty for taking sensible measures to monitor your child, even if it appears that you are not treating your child as trustworthy. It is particularly important that you should not 'test' your child's trustworthiness by putting him in a situation of risk to see what happens. It would not be sensible to put a bottle in front of a person who is recovering from being an alcoholic to see if he or she would drink it. In the same way, it is not a good idea to give your child opportunities which involve risk in order to see if he will abuse again.

A second question is, 'how do I trust my child after this has happened?' Often parents say that they want to trust their child again but simply do not feel able to. If you are feeling this way, it may be a good indicator that you still need to be cautious and watchful. A third question is 'If I trust him will he abuse my trust?' It is important to avoid falling into 'all-or-nothing' thinking about trust. Trusting your child is not, and should not be, something you do as a one-off. Just because you trust your child in one situation does not mean to say you should trust him in all others. Trust needs to be earned. Your child can gain your trust by accepting responsibility and showing you that he can respond to this positively.

Forgiveness is not the same as trust. You can forgive your child for the pain that the abuse has caused you and the disruption to your life and that of your family, without having to feel absolute trust of your child in all situations. Whether and when to forgive is for you to decide. Forgiving your child will also have different meanings for different people. Remember that if you forgive, you can only do this for the pain and impact that the abuse has caused you. You cannot forgive your child on behalf of others, for example the victim of the abuse. Even if you decide to forgive your child, this should not mean that the abuse does not matter any more. Forgiving does not mean forgetting. Indeed, forgetting about the abuse (or pretending that it did not happen) is rarely a safe strategy.

Managing feelings about sexual abusers

Dealing with your child's sexually abusive behaviour may also mean that you have to confront your own attitudes and beliefs about sexual abusers. You may have read things about sex offenders in the newspapers, where the whole issue of people who commit sex offences is often dealt with in an unhelpful way. Sex offenders are often described as 'monsters' or 'beasts' and the message is that such people should be locked up, the key thrown away and that they should never be given another chance. There may have been no reason for you to have considered these simplistic and often misinformed messages in any more depth before. Parents sometimes find it hard to reconcile the beliefs they have held about 'paedophiles' in the past with their feelings about their own child. This can create a belief dilemma for a parent. Should you hold onto a belief that sexual abusers are evil and see your child in this way, or should you maintain a view that your child is basically good, but has done something badly wrong?

Coping with depression

Most of us feel down or depressed at some point in our lives, especially when we face problems that seem too difficult to cope with. The impact of having a child who has sexually abused may well send a parent into depression, even if you have no history of this previously. When you are depressed you may feel especially bad about yourself, and lonely or isolated or hopeless. Depression is a medical condition which can be diagnosed by a doctor. It is often classified as either 'mild', 'moderate', or 'severe', depending upon the symptoms and their effect. If a person has mild depression, the symptoms may not last very long and may have little effect on how the person manages or copes with everyday life. On the other hand, if a person has moderate to severe depression there are likely to be symptoms that are stronger, last longer and tend to have a bad effect on the things that the person does on a day-to-day basis.

Many of the parents I have worked with experience depression. If you have depression you should not feel ashamed of this. Some of the typical symptoms of depression include:

- feeling down or empty
- having a lack of interest in things or pleasure
- feeling that life is hopeless
- thinking about suicide
- feeling worthless as a person or guilty
- feeling like you can't be bothered
- not being able to concentrate on things
- not being able to sleep
- not eating: having no appetite

If you think that you are suffering from depression or if the symptoms listed above are familiar to you, then you should consider seeing your doctor and talking this through. As a rough guide, answer the following questions:

- Have you lost interest and pleasure in things you usually enjoy?
- Have you lost energy or do you feel over-tired?
- Are you feeling sad or down?
- Have you noticed a change in your sleep patterns?
- Are you more moody and irritable than usual?
- Do you feel that your life is hopeless?

If you have answered yes to one or more of these questions, especially if this has been how you have felt over a prolonged period, you may wish to consult your GP. Your doctor will be able to advise you and may be able to refer you to a counsellor or give you other appropriate medical help, including medication in more severe cases. Other tips for dealing with feeling down or depressed include:

- Build some routine or structure into your day. Try setting yourself some daily goals. This can be especially valuable if your child is no longer living with you and your routine as a family, or role as a parent, has been disturbed as a result.

- Do something that you enjoy. It is all too easy to withdraw into yourself once the sexual abuse has become known. Remember that doing something for yourself is still OK, even though you and your family may be in crisis. If you can maintain some kind of interest or activity, you are more likely to be able to help your child. It is important though, not to over-do things, or over-stretch yourself.

- Get support. Even if the supporter does not know everything about the abuse, having someone to spend time with and talk to can help you keep a balance and to remember that there are things out in the world other than sexual abuse.

- Rest and sleep. Some parents find it very hard to sleep and lie awake thinking about things or worrying about what might happen in their house if they go to sleep. However, rest and sleep are necessary for you to meet the challenges you face in the day. If you are finding it difficult to relax or sleep, try the relaxation exercises suggested later in this chapter. At the same time, it is important not to overdo sleep. Eight hours each day should be enough.

- Eat healthily and don't miss out meals. Avoid drinking too much alcohol as this tends to make people feel worse rather than better.

- Do some physical exercise. This can refresh you, help you think clearly and keep you going during the difficult times.

- Do not cut off from your feelings. Allow yourself to express them but find safe times and safe ways of doing this.

- Notice and correct any negative or hopeless messages in your head, for example, 'there's no hope', or, 'what's the point'. Remind yourself that there can be a future beyond the sexual abuse. Give yourself positive messages. Try writing them down and displaying them somewhere appropriate in your home so that you can remind yourself of them when you are at your lowest. For example, one mother who was in a parents' support group wrote down a possitive comment that another mother said to her, then she kept this note by her bed to look at when she felt really down.

Coping with 'flashbacks' or nightmares

What is a flashback?

A flashback is a sudden memory of a traumatic event earlier in a person's life which comes back into mind and intrudes into everyday life. If you have a flashback it may be as if you are experiencing the original incident all over again in front of your eyes. They can vary in length and strength.

Flashbacks are often experienced by adults who have experienced sexual abuse when they were children. They can happen without warning and the person experiencing the flashback may not be aware that it is happening until it is over. They may be triggered by something that has been said or something you have seen, a gesture or a word that someone has used that reminds you of the traumatic event. They can also be triggered by a particular smell, or a touch. Flashbacks can be extremely concerning and can make people experiencing them feel as afraid and out of control as they felt during the original traumatic event itself. Flashbacks can also take the form of disturbing nightmares.

Why are flashbacks relevant to parents?

I have included a discussion on flashbacks for several important reasons.

Firstly, it is important for you to be aware that victims may experience flashbacks. This demonstrates the power that the abuser can continue to have even after the abuse has ended and the ongoing damage that can be created by experiencing sexual abuse. If you have a child in your family who is a victim of sexual abuse, or if the young person who has abused has also been the victim of sexual abuse in the past, you should be aware that there may be times when the child is reminded of the abuse and may experience a flashback. Some signs of a child or young person having a flashback may include:

- The child's eyes glazing over and the child seeming lost in thought.
- The child not responding, or acting as if they aren't there any more.
- The child suddenly becoming distressed and emotional (although this may also be a sign of an ongoing problem).

Things you can do in these situations are:

- Remove the things that are likely to trigger flashbacks.
- Talk to the child calmly, looking into the child's eyes, repeating where she is and who else is there, e.g. 'Jenny, you are here in the house with mummy and you are safe, there is no one else here...'.

The second reason for including discussion on flashbacks is that the young person who has abused may experience a flashback to a time when they abused their victim. Young people may find themselves in a situation where they are reminded about the abuse, or see, smell or hear something that brings pictures of the abuse back into their minds. Sometimes this can create a sexual response from young people who can feel themselves becoming sexually aroused. This may be very confusing and upsetting to a young person who is working hard to stop abusing, for example:

> Mike, aged 17, had abused five young children including his siblings and their friends. He had been through group and individual therapy for almost two years and was nearing the end of this. He was deeply committed to leading a life without abuse, had a girlfriend and was doing well at college. At certain times when was at home, pictures of the abuse would come back into his head, he would start to get an erection and he would become deeply distressed.

In situations like the one for Mike, specialist professional involvement may be required to help the young person change his patterns of sexual arousal. However, if Mike could have talked to his parents when he had these feelings at home, even if their response had been simply to tell him that they were proud that he had been working to stop abusing, this could have been a significant support to him.

The third reason I include discussion of flashbacks is that I have become increasingly aware from parents that they can also experience intrusive thoughts or pictures about their child's abuse, either whilst awake or in nightmares. If this is the case for you, you can try the following ways of coping with a flashback:

- Tell yourself you are having a flashback and that this is normal in parents who are coping with their child's sexual abuse.

- If your flashback or nightmare involves the victim being abused or in some kind of distress, tell the child (in your imagination) that she is not alone any more and that you will help.

- Remind yourself where you are, who you are and what you are trying to do in order to prevent further abuse as a parent.

- Slow your breathing down and try to relax, especially if the flashback leaves you feeling panicky or short of breath. The relaxation exercises later in this chapter may help you.

- If you have the support of a partner, talk to them about what happens to you when you have intrusive pictures or 'flashbacks' in your head. Ask your partner to be there for you and talk to you to give you positive messages at these times. Talking about this in advance will help your partner be aware of how best to help or comfort you.

Dealing with your own sexual abuse as a child

If you have experienced abuse in your own past, it may be that memories of this abuse have been reawakened by the discovery of your own child's sexually abusive behaviour. This may be true regardless of the type of abuse in your past, but it can be particularly painful if you experienced sexual abuse. It is not unusual for adults who were abused as children to have memories of their experiences 'triggered' by something in their adulthood. You may experience flashbacks to experiences you tried to forget long ago. For some parents, their child's sexually abusive behaviour and their learning more about sexual abuse may have led them to realise or acknowledge to themselves for the very first time that they were abused as a child. Even if you have clear memories of your experiences of sexual abuse as a child, you may never have told anyone about this and you may not have been given any help with your experiences.

If you are still unsure as to whether you have experienced sexual abuse, think about the following questions:

- Has anyone ever (i.e. either when you were a child, teenager or adult) forced or tricked you into doing something sexual against your will?

- Before the age of 16 years old, did someone who was an adult, especially if they were in a position of authority over you involve you in any kind of sexual act?

- When you were a child, did anyone ever encourage you to do something sexual about which you were unsure, which you did not really understand, or the consequences of which were beyond your understanding?

- When you were a child, did an older child do anything sexual to you which made you feel uncomfortable, upset or stop you from making other relationships?

If you have answered yes to any of these questions, it is likely that you are a survivor of sexual abuse. The word 'survivor' refers to an adult who was sexually abused as a child. It does not imply that you no longer feel upset or hurt by the abuse. Both men and women can be abuse survivors.

If you are a survivor of sexual abuse you may feel that your child's sexually abusive behaviour has victimised you all over again. It is important for you to remember that you were not to blame for the sexual abuse which you experienced. Survivors can often feel that they were responsible and have feelings of deep guilt and shame which persist well into adulthood. Sometimes, this is clearly linked to what the abuser said to you as a child in order to make you feel guilty or afraid and unable to tell other people. Survivors can feel that they were to blame because their bodies responded to the abuse and they became aroused or had an orgasm during the abuse. Abusers often use this as a way of making a child feel responsible for the abuse, when in fact this is just a body's automatic way of responding when touched. It does not mean that the victim was 'enjoying' what was being done.

All survivors' experiences of sexual abuse and the consequences of the abuse are in some ways unique. However, adults sexually abused in childhood often are left with some of the following feelings and behaviours:

- Feeling bad or having a low opinion of themselves.
- Feeling bad about their bodies and not enjoying a fulfilling sex life.
- Feeling depressed about their lives.
- Experiencing sleep problems or nightmares about the abuse.
- Finding it difficult to trust other people.
- Finding yourself in situations where you are sexually hurt by partners.
- Experiencing flashbacks to your abuse when you are awake.
- Having problems controlling feelings of anger.
- Having problems with drugs, alcohol, eating problems or disorders or self-harmful behaviours.
- Feeling overwhelmed or flooded with difficult emotions.

Often survivors also develop many positive assets and strengths. This is not because of the abuse, but because of the survivor's effort and courage in coming to terms with her experiences. Many survivors I have been privileged to talk to about their abuse are amongst the strongest and most caring people I have met. In many cases, survivors are very creative people and many are committed to ending child abuse for others. However, if you are left with some of the difficult emotions and feelings I have listed above, do not blame yourself or think that you are weak for not being able to put the abuse behind you. These are natural responses to the abuse experiences you have had as a child and are understandable. You should not feel that your life has necessarily been ruined by the abuse. You can gain your life back. For example, Laura was a mother whose step-daughter sexually abused her two other children. When she found out about this, she realised she needed help to overcome her own sexual abuse as a child and she found a place in a local survivors' support group. Hearing about other people's experiences of surviving abuse, and receiving their support, gave Laura the confidence she needed to begin to help her step-daughter.

If you are only now acknowledging your abuse or its effects upon you as a result of your child's abusive behaviours, you should think about getting some help for yourself from a trained counsellor who is experienced in working with adult survivors of abuse. If this is not possible for you at the present time, you could get hold of some of the self-help books written for survivors of abuse. Two of the best-known are:

- *The Courage to Heal: A Guide for Women Survivors of Child Sexual Abuse* by Ellen Bass and Laura Davis, published in 1988 by Harper and Row, New York.
- *Victims No Longer. A Guide for Men Recovering from Sexual Child Abuse* by Mike Lew, published in 1993 by Cedar, London.

If you would like to ring someone to talk about your experiences, you could contact your local rape crisis centre, whose phone number should be listed in the phonebook. You could also ring one of a number of national telephone helplines which can offer advice and support, such as the Samaritans (08457 90 90 90). If you feel you can entrust this information to a social worker or other professional involved in your child's life currently, this person should be able to point you in the direction of good local services for survivors.

Remember that seeking help to recover from childhood sexual abuse is a sign of strength not weakness, and that, even though your abuser may have told you differently, a counsellor will believe you and take your experiences, and any consequences they have had for your life, seriously.

Some survivors may still have contact with the person who has abused them when they were a child, especially if this person is a relative, for instance a father or older brother. If this is the case for you, it is important that you make sure that this person does not continue to abuse or hurt you. You should also take steps to ensure that this person does not have unsupervised access to your children, as we have already seen in Chapter 3 how sexually abusive behaviour can be addictive and can continue over many years, especially if the person concerned has not been offered help.

Relaxation techniques

Dealing with the issues created by your child's sexual abuse can be extremely stressful. Parents can experience a range of physical stress symptoms including physical exhaustion, body pains and headaches. One mother I worked with said she found it impossible to relax and was 'on edge' for most of the time. If you feel like this, it is worth practising some relaxation techniques to see if they can help. You may feel that these are a little strange at first and you may feel slightly embarrassed, but it is worth persevering with them. They are also better for you than other destructive ways of dealing with stress, like drinking too much alcohol, hurting yourself or taking your aggression out on someone.

Relaxation Exercise One: Tensing and relaxing your muscles

- Loosen any tight clothes and get yourself into a comfortable position. Close your eyes if you like.
- Tighten the muscles in your toes. Hold for ten seconds. Relax and try to feel the relaxation spreading out from your toes.
- Tighten the muscles in your feet. Hold for ten seconds. Relax.
- Move slowly up through your body: your legs, stomach, chest, arms, hands, back, neck, face in turn: tightening and relaxing the muscles as you go. Pay particular attention to any area of your body which feels tense.
- Breathe deeply and slowly as you do this.
- If you like, when you feel totally relaxed you can think of positive messages for yourself, such as 'I will get through this' or 'there is a future beyond these problems'.
- Finish the exercise by shaking out your hands and arms and imagining all the tension flowing out of your fingertips.

Relaxation Exercise Two: Breathing

- Loosen any tight clothes and get yourself into a comfortable position with your arms by your side.
- Close your eyes and breathe deeply. Make your breathing be slow and relaxed.
- Focus all your attention on your breathing and be aware of the movement of your chest and stomach, in and out.
- Block out all other thoughts, feelings, and sensations. If you feel yourself thinking about anything else, concentrate on slowing down your breathing.
- When you are feeling totally relaxed, you can repeat positive words to yourself such as 'strength' or 'hope' as you breathe in and out, or you can imagine yourself in a peaceful or calming place.

Dealing with the Impact of your Child's Behaviour on your Relationship

Given that the sexual abuse can have such an impact upon an individual parent, it is hardly surprising that the stresses, demands and emotions often also put pressure on even the best relationships between partners. This means that you should also take some time and pay particular attention to your relationship, not only because of the impact it has upon children in your family (although that is undoubtedly important), but also for the sake of the relationship itself. Even if you are in a strong, loving and equal relationship, your child's sexually abusive behaviour can shift the focus away from this onto other matters. You can be so busy with looking after your children, attending meetings, monitoring and supervising situations, that you can let your relationship needs become secondary. All relationships, even good ones, need to be sustained.

It is common for parents whose children have engaged in sexually abusive behaviour to experience some kind of impact upon their own sex lives. Parents who are in a sexual relationship may be put off sex for a time and may start to think of sex as dirty or distasteful. Parents who are not currently in a relationship may find it harder to think about or go about establishing one. In other cases, parents can start to question their own sexual behaviours and sexuality. Sexually problematic behaviour and abuse thrives on secrecy and unequal relationships. Therefore, keeping your own sex life healthy after your child's abuse is discovered is easiest when you can talk about your feelings, sexual thoughts and needs with your sexual partner.

Sex is an important part of adult relationships: it should be enjoyable and shared. Do not neglect the sexual part of you because of the sexual abuse. If there are things that you realise were already wrong with your sex life and relationship before you found out about the abuse, try to use this as a good opportunity to deal with these issues now. Sex following abuse can also be an area which exposes differences in feelings between men and women in relationships. It may be important to review your sex life and to talk about your feelings about sex and your needs even if you have long-established and happy sex lives. Be careful to accept that your partner now may have different feelings and a different perspective on sex due to what has happened. Some parents can experience flashbacks or intrusive images to the abuse whilst they are having sex, so a great deal of sensitivity and support is needed.

There are also more straightforward practical difficulties which can cause problems in relation to keeping your relationship healthy. Simply going out as a couple may pose practical difficulties. You can be faced with decisions such as who to leave your children with and how to respond to the increased issues of safety that the abuse brings. The babysitting arrangements you used to have may no longer be appropriate, especially if they involved teenagers. You may also feel very drained with the emotional and practical demands of parenting in situations following abuse and having enough energy left to be able to keep your relationship healthy may not feel like a priority. One thing you can try is to do at least one thing each week that you enjoy as a couple.

Summary points from this section

- Your own needs are important, even if other people in your family are relying upon you to meet their needs.
- You are likely to experience emotional ups and downs.
- Your child's sexual abuse can reawaken painful memories from your past, or may cause you to think back and reassess your own childhood.
- A child's sexual abuse can place stresses and pressure on relationships.

Questions to consider

- What are your own needs and what ways can you identify to meet them?
- What can you do to ensure that you have some support, space and time for yourself, whilst at the same time not leaving others more vulnerable or unsafe?
- How can you ensure that your relationship is a source of support?

Exercise 11: Meeting your own needs and getting support

Purpose. This exercise is designed to help you to consider your own needs following the abuse and to identify ways in which you may be able to meet these needs.

1. What are the practical supports I need to cope with day-to-day life?

....

....

....

....

2. What are my emotional needs?

....

....

....

....

3. What can I do myself to meet these needs?

....

....

....

....

4. What can other people do? Which other people?

....

....

....

....

5. If these needs are met, I will be in a stronger position to:

....

....

....

....

Chapter 5

Making Changes and Protecting Others in your Family

Creating Positive Changes in your Family

Many parents ask whether their family is typical of families where children have sexually abused. In reality, young people who have sexually abused come from all kinds of families and these families have all kinds of strengths and difficulties. You should weigh up the particularly good and not so good things about your family. Doing this will give you an opportunity to think about how you might improve the strengths and reduce the difficulties.

There is a fine line between saying that certain family problems tend to be seen in families where sexual abuse occurs, and at the same time making sure that parents are not blamed for their child's behaviour. The responsibility for the sexual abuse needs to be given to your child, but this should not stop you from making positive and necessary changes to your family. As parents, seeing that we should have done better in something is never easy and this applies very strongly to situations where sexual abuse has taken place. Parents can use the realisation that something was not quite right in their families in the past to make appropriate and necessary life changes. Here are three examples taken from parents I have worked with:

1. Alan's mother and father realised that they had given Alan (aged 16) far too much responsibility for looking after his younger brothers and sisters. He had become their 'parent' and this had stopped him developing proper relationships with people his own age. It also gave him lots of opportunities to abuse them. After the abuse came out in the open Alan's parents realised that they needed to take back the responsibility for their younger children.

2. Jerome's mother was concerned that she might have encouraged Jerome to abuse his younger brother as they had always shared a bed together since being toddlers. She decided that she needed help with her parenting skills and with the help of her social worker was able to find a local parenting class. Here she met other mothers and was able to begin to share her experiences and learn from others about the challenges of being a single carer of two boys.

3. Paul's mother had lived with her husband's beatings and verbal abuse for many years before Paul's abuse was discovered. She realised that her husband's violence had been very damaging to Paul and his brothers and had made them believe that it was normal for men to hurt and put down women. She decided that it was time for her to make a break from this violent relationship both for her own sake, but also to give Paul the best chance of stopping abusing and to show him that it was possible to change.

In all of the examples above the parents involved felt that they had failed their children in some way. Although they were not responsible for their children's behaviours, the changes that they were able to make were all necessary in order to give their children the best chance of success in their treatment work.

Some studies have tried to look at what is common in families where children have sexually abused or have compared the family experiences of young people who have sexually abused against those of other young people. In summarising below some of the main points from these studies (see Calder, 2001), I hope to encourage parents to look at their own families and to see whether they need to make changes in relation to any of these factors. It is worth remembering that there are good and not-so-good qualities in most families, and that these qualities can and do change over time in response to stress and other difficulties. However, these are some of the key problems often found in families where children have sexually abused:

- Relationships between parents and children that are distant or without emotional closeness.
- Children seeing difficulties between parents, in particular physical violence from one parent to the other (usually a man being violent to a woman).
- Children experiencing physical violence from a parent.
- Lots of family changes or breakdown, with children being cared for by different people.
- Fathers who take little or no responsibility for parenting.
- Family roles being blurred, especially: children taking on too much responsibility, older children being treated as babies, etc.
- Family roles which are swapped: for example, where the child becomes the parent and the parent becomes the child.
- Lack of warmth in the way that the adults in the family treat the children.
- A lack of supervision of children by parents (parents often not knowing what the children are doing and where they are).
- Lack of openness in the family: lots of unhealthy family secrets.
- Parents setting the children a poor example through their behaviour, for example criminal behaviour.
- Parents who have been abused as children but who have not come to terms with this as adults.
- Children seeing siblings or parents having sex in the family.
- A sexual environment in the family; where sex is everywhere.
- Family rules that are too strict and stop the children developing e.g. all sex is bad, etc.
- Patterns of sexual abuse that stretch back over generations.

If you have gone through the list above and picked out any points which are true for your family, you may wish to consider how you might change the way your family operates, to reduce the negative effects of these points. The exercise later in this section entitled *Family Change Factors* may help with this. Some particular suggestions based on the lessons learnt from other families include **paying careful attention to your family roles**. It may be important to look carefully at who does what in your family and how you could change this to make sure that the roles are appropriate. If there are two adults in your home who care for the children, it is important to consider how you can **share the childcare fairly** between you. In working with parents whose children have sexually abused, it has often been the case that mothers have taken on most or all of the responsibilities for childcare before and after the abuse. Even if this was acceptable for a mother before the abuse, it simply is not fair for women to be left doing everything after the abuse has come to light. There are likely to be extra parenting tasks to monitor situations and deal with risky situations in your family. In such situations, it is vital that fathers who may not have ever considered themselves to be directly responsible for child care activities are willing to take some of this pressure off mothers. It is also important to **look again at family rules and boundaries,** especially those about sex and body privacy. Perhaps the single most important change you can make is to sort out **family safety issues**. This involves doing all you can to ensure that there are no opportunities in your family for the abuse to continue in any way. Advice on how to do this is offered later in this chapter.

If you know or suspect an adult in your family is a sexual abuser

Through the process of facing up to their child's abusive behaviour, some parents realise or face up to the fact, perhaps for the first time, that an adult in their family has a history of sexually abusive behaviour.

If this person has never been challenged about his behaviour and has never had help, there is a good possibility that he is still abusing. This person may be caught in a cycle of abuse that has lasted for many years. Indeed, you may be wondering whether your child has been abused by this person in the past. You may also feel uncertain as to what to do, especially if it is your father, grandfather, uncle, cousin, etc. It is, however, not fair that your child is faced with the consequences of his behaviour when the other, older person is not. In such circumstances you should quickly:

- Stop any abuse that you know or suspect is happening.
- Take action to protect others who may be vulnerable or at risk from this person (e.g. stop this person from caring for or looking after children).
- Report the abuser (to local police or social services).

Remember that covering up for the person because of family loyalties leaves others at risk and is not in the interests of the abuser, who will not get the help he needs.

If the person has already been given help and has been reported in the past, it is still important for you to limit the opportunities that this person has to abuse again. This means not allowing this person to have access to your children, including the child who has abused, especially when you are not there. Just because the child who has abused has behaved in a sexually harmful way to others does not, of course, mean that he is himself immune from being abused.

If you suspect that someone who has already been reported (and possibly convicted) of abuse in the past has started to abuse again, report this person again. If in any doubt about who to ring in your area, you can try the NSPCC helpline on 0808 800 5000 which is a national freephone number. Counsellors there will be able to advise you, put you in touch with local services and pass information on to the relevant people for you.

If you are being hurt or abused in your relationship

As a parent, if you are being battered, hurt or abused physically, sexually or emotionally by your partner, this is commonly known as domestic violence. The simple message is to get help. The national domestic violence helpline number is 0345 023468.

In heterosexual relationships (a man and a woman as partners or married) it is nearly always a woman who is on the receiving end of domestic violence and a man who is abusing. Many women who experience domestic violence suffer it in silence for years. Some mothers feel that they are unable to free themselves from this abuse because they are frightened of the consequences or because they feel that it is their duty to keep the family together. However, domestic violence is unacceptable and you should not have to put up with this. It is also questionable whether a family where one parent (usually the father) is being violent to the other can provide a stable or safe enough platform for your child's recovery after abuse. If nothing else, witnessing domestic violence provides a very bad example to the young person who has sexually abused about the way that men treat women and the 'acceptability' of physical violence, as can be seen below:

> Madge had lived with her physically violent husband for many years. Her eldest son had grown up to physically abuse his mother too. Her youngest son, Lee, had also been very frightened of his father. Lee sexually abused several children in the neighbourhood. Whilst in a group for parents whose children had abused, Madge was able to talk about her experiences of domestic violence for the first time and received lots of messages of support. She realised that if she wanted to help her son recover after the abuse, she needed to end the domestic violence. After seeking advice from a domestic violence counsellor, she ended the relationship with her husband. Later she described this as the best thing she had ever done and she felt like she had gained her self respect back. She was able to have Lee come back and live with her again and to support his treatment work.

Some women need time to make the kind of changes Madge was able to make. Other women choose not to leave their partner. Whatever your experiences are, getting the help of someone who knows about domestic violence and who can tell you what services are available for you in your local area is important.

Summary points from this section

- There are some common factors associated with families where children have sexually abused. If any of these factors apply to your family, it may help your child (and other children) if these could be made more positive.
- Families usually have good and bad bits: strengths and weaknesses. It is important to build on the strengths and take away as many of the bad points as is possible.
- Family change doesn't just happen overnight but is a long-term process. Start with the positive things you can change and work on those that are not so easy.
- Making it safe, for yourself as a parent and for your children, is a vital first step in wider family change.

Questions to consider

- How many of the common factors listed above, from studies of families where children have abused, apply to your family? (see also Exercise 14)
- What could be changed immediately and what needs more time and effort?
- How can you begin to make these changes? Who needs to take the lead on these points?
- Are there safety issues that need to be resolved in your family first of all?

Exercise 12: Family strengths and weaknesses

Purpose. This exercise is designed to help you identify the strengths and weaknesses in your family and the things you can change to increase the strengths.

1. In the left hand column make a list of the strengths or 'good things' about your family and below this the weaknesses or 'not-so-good' things about your family.

2. On the right hand side, write down for each point who would agree with you that this is a strength or weakness.

• Family strengths	• Who would agree?
• Family weaknesses	• Who would agree?

3. List ideas you have about how to increase the strengths and decrease the weaknesses.

....

....

4. What would be different if your family could make these improvements?

....

....

5. Who would benefit from the changes in particular?

....

....

Exercise 13: Caring by two: making it fair

Purpose. If you share with another person the care of a child who has abused, this exercise is designed to help you to think of your role in the family and how you can support each other.

Even if the young person who abused does not live with you on a full-time basis and just visits, this can place severe stress on parents who need to make sure that any time the young person spends in the family he (and the community) is safe.

Each parent or carer should fill in their own part of this exercise separately then discuss what they have written with their partner. Number 3 should then be completed together.

1. Carer One

My role in the family is:

....

....

....

Things I do are:

....

....

....

What I do or have done about the sexual abuse is:

....

....

....

Things I would like to share some more are:

....

....

....

I could be better supported if:

....

....

....

2. Carer Two

My role in the family is:

....

....

Things I do are:

....

....

What I do or have done about the sexual abuse is:

....

....

Things I would like to share some more are:

....

....

I could be better supported if:

....

....

3. Together

What we can agree to change to make it fairer:

....

....

Things to share more equally:

....

....

How to help each other when one of us is feeling down:

....

....

What needs to change in our relationship:

....

....

How we can organise our daily life differently:

....

....

Other responsibilities we can agree to share differently or more fairly:

....

....

Exercise 14: Family change factors

Purpose. This exercise is designed to help you think about what changes it is important to make in your family and how to go about making such changes.

1. On the left hand side you will find a list of things that commonly need to change in families where a child has sexually abused. For each of the points or 'change factors', use the middle column to write down what your family is like in respect of this point. The final box is to score how important it is in your family to make some changes to each issue. Nought out of ten would mean that you have absolutely nothing to change, ten out of ten would suggest that it is absolutely vital to change this in your family.

Family change factor	What my family is like for this point	Change importance score (0–10)
Relationships between parents and children that are distant or without closeness		
Physical violence from one parent to the other (usually male being violent to the female)		
Children experiencing physical violence from a parent		
Lots of family changes or breakdown, with children being cared for by different people		
Fathers who take little or no responsibility for parenting		
Family roles being blurred, especially children taking on too much responsibility, older children being treated as babies, etc.		
Family roles which are swapped: for example, where the child becomes the parent and the parent becomes the child in some way		
Lack of warmth in the way that the adults in the family treat the children		
A lack of supervision of children by parents (parents often not knowing what the children are doing)		

Lack of openness in the family, lots of unhealthy family secrets		
Parents setting the children a poor example through their behaviour, for example, criminal behaviour		
Parents who have been abused as children but who haven't come to terms with this as adults		
Children seeing siblings or parents having sex in the family		
A sexual environment in the family, sex is everywhere		
Family rules that are too strict and stop the children developing, e.g. all sex is bad, etc.		
Patterns of sexual abuse that stretch back over generations		

2. Review your list. Pick out the five change factors that scored the highest and write them down in order of their score. For each, write down who can take the lead in making the change and who else needs to help.

Order of importance	Who can take the lead? How should the change be made?	Who else needs to help make the change?
Highest score		
Second highest score		
Third highest score		
Fourth highest score		
Fifth highest score		

Better Parenting Now and in the Future

Your child's sexually abusive behaviour does not mean that you should consider yourself to be a bad parent. However, there may be areas of your parenting which you could usefully develop in order to give the best possible support to the young person who has abused and to other children who may be in your family. Chapter 6 goes into detail about the specific things that you can do to take part in any work being offered to your child. The next section in this chapter discusses how you can deal with risk situations in your home and community. However, this section briefly sets down some of the key points about parenting all children, with some of my thoughts about the importance of these points for young people who have sexually abused. You should remember that there is no such thing as a perfect parent or a perfect family. All parents experience stress and difficulties that sometimes mean that their parenting suffers. Just because the abuse happened, this does not wipe out all the good things about your parenting, your family and your child. The important thing is to have an understanding of what you should strive for in your parenting in the future and an idea of how you can achieve these goals.

Parenting styles and skills

Studies suggest (e.g. Baumrind, 1991) that effective parenting is a mixture of firm discipline in the face of a child's difficult behaviour, whilst responding to the child's needs consistently, at all other times. Importantly, it is the presence of **both** of these qualities together that seem to help children to develop into well-adjusted people (Strand, 2000). In other words, being strict and a 'disciplinarian' when your child does something wrong without being warm and taking an interest in other aspects of your child's life, does not help. Similarly, being warm and supportive without expecting your child to behave appropriately is not ideal.

Effective parenting is not just about disciplining your child when things go wrong. It is also about recognising the positive things your child does, such as when your child achieves something, behaves well or shares personal experiences with you. Most importantly of all, effective parenting means being **predictable** towards your children from day to day, so that they know how you are likely to respond if they behave well or badly, and so on.

So, some important elements of effective parenting are:

1. Improving the overall quality of your relationship with your child.

2. Helping children develop good feelings or self esteem about themselves.

3. Developing good ways of listening and communicating with your child.

4. Using discipline properly without resorting to physical punishment.

5. Setting boundaries for your children and helping them to develop appropriate ways of behaving.

6. Having fun times with your children.

1. Improving the overall quality of your relationship with your child

Studies show that one of the most important factors in adolescents' well-being is the quality of the relationship they have with their parents (Barber and Delfabbro, 2000). Improving the overall quality of your relationship with your child is at least as important as developing specific parenting skills. This involves:

- Reducing the overall level of conflict in your relationship. This doesn't mean just giving in to your child! It is about looking at the situations that lead to conflict and thinking about how to deal with these situations in a different way (see Exercise 15).

- Being there as a consistent source of support for your children so that they can explore the world around them safely.

2. Helping your children to develop self esteem

One of the most important aspects of parenting is to help children feel that they are worth something as people, that they are liked and are 'likeable'. In order to develop into sensitive and caring adults, children need to feel that they are accepted, loved, understood and appreciated by their parents. This just does not happen overnight but is a long-term process. One argument with your children will not ruin their sense of self-esteem, but constant criticism and harsh treatment will.

You can help develop your children's self-esteem by showing an interest in them and by spending time with them. However, encouraging positive self-esteem is not about just letting children do what they want to without any boundaries or rules. You should direct your children and be a 'guide' for them in their learning about the world. When you put controls around what your children should do, you should do this in a caring way, so that their self-esteem is not undermined or destroyed. This helps children to see that they also have some control in their own lives. By the time they are adolescents, they need to know that they have some freedom to make choices and that they should take responsibility for the decisions they make.

For young people who have sexually abused, regaining self-esteem (or for some young people gaining it for the first time) is a crucial aspect of trying to live a life free of abusive behaviour. We have seen in Chapter 3 that some young people's low self-esteem can be directly linked to their decision to sexually abuse, so raising their self-esteem is a key task for parents and professionals alike. Being caught as a result of their abusive behaviour is also likely to further reduce their self-esteem and they can very easily come to believe very negative thoughts about themselves, for example as 'dirty', 'evil' or 'perverts', etc. In such cases, it is important that young people receive consistent messages from their parents which take the abuse seriously and help them recover their feelings of self-worth. If your child feels totally ashamed of himself and has no sense of self worth, this is not a good starting point for making the kind of major changes that are necessary after abusive behaviour. The following points may provide useful ways of encouraging your child to be accountable for the abuse, whilst at the same time, promoting a positive and non-abusive sense of self:

- You should be clear with your child that you do not like what he has done, but that does not mean to say that you do not love him. In this way, you are separating out the child's sexually abusive behaviour from him as a person.

- You should be positive about the good things about your child's overall behaviour and you should let your child know what you believe these good points to be. A young person's behaviour is rarely all bad.

- If your child is accepting help and working hard in a treatment programme to address his behaviour, you should reinforce this by saying that he is showing courage by facing up to the abuse and, however hard this is, that you feel proud of him for this.

- You should let your child know that you believe that he can succeed. In other words, he can lead an abuse-free life in the future and need not consider himself as a 'sex offender' for the rest of his life. Few young people will make the effort to undergo difficult work if the message they receive from those around them is that it will not make any difference.

As well as making the above statements consistently to your child, there are also likely to be a number of practical things that you can **do** to help your child increase his self-esteem and self-belief. Again, these must be balanced with the need to protect others and to develop ways of dealing with risky situations. To give your child a say in decision-making and to consult him about things affecting him is important. Allowing your child to get things right or succeed in things is a good strategy, as is praising your child for things he gets right. The following case example demonstrates how success in one part of a young person's life can have a knock-on effect in others:

> David, aged sixteen, was so shy and shameful about his sexually abusive behaviour and his confidence was so shattered that he couldn't look people in the eye. He was part of a groupwork programme for young men who had sexually abused but was so under confident that he hardly spoke. At home, he withdrew into himself which was what had happened before he had sexually abused. By chance, the group leaders found out that David enjoyed cooking. He was encouraged to plan a meal for the group and given money to go to the shops to buy the food. He cooked the meal for the group and this was a great success. David was proud of himself and the other group members were really impressed. Later, David enrolled in a catering course at college where he made a circle of friends his own age for the first time in his adolescence.

3. Developing good ways of listening and communicating with your child

Communicating well with children is more than just about what we say. We also communicate a lot to children by our behaviour. Children and young people can be very skilled at exposing the differences between what an adult says and does. Communication is a two-way process. It is what you communicate **to** your child and what you understand and receive **from** your child. This involves developing listening skills as a parent. Very often children do not tell us in words how they are feeling and we need to be sensitive to the messages being communicated by the child's actions. Be aware that children at different stages of development communicate in different ways. Young children communicate through play. Spending time playing with younger children is often a good way of giving them an opportunity to show you through their play what is on their mind. Teenagers can find it difficult to talk to parents about their feelings and often do not appreciate being put under pressure to answer direct questions.

4. Using discipline properly without resorting to physical punishment

I distinguish between **discipline** and **physical punishment** because studies show that it is important to **discipline** children, by which I mean doing something to discourage negative behaviours and more generally putting limits around what our children can and cannot do. However trying to discipline children by resorting to physical punishment, smacking or hitting, does not work for a number of reasons. In particular, physical punishment tries to control children's behaviour by making them scared of the consequences of a particular behaviour rather than by helping them to develop a conscience. Worse still, trying to control children and young people by hitting them can make the child believe that it is OK to use physical force and fear to control others. In other words, children can end up thinking that the behaviour which they have 'got into trouble about' is OK because of the physical punishment they have received. For example a child might think 'why should I stop hurting my sister if my dad and mum hurt me?' Children also tend to base their ways of coping with situations on how they see their parents behaving in similar situations. So, if your child sees you hitting out when under pressure or stressed, they can copy this.

Studies of parents' use of discipline (Strand, 2000) highlight the following points:

- Explaining the reasoning for what is correct behaviour and what is not has been shown to be more effective than punishment alone.

- If you have a close, warm and caring relationship with your child then your child is much more likely to listen to you and do as you say. Physical punishment tends to alienate children from parents and make them less likely to come to you for help.

- Discipline is found to be more effective the sooner it happens following an unacceptable behaviour.

- Parents need to be consistent with their ways of disciplining.

- Children are more likely to respond to the ways a parent chooses to discipline them if these have been explained calmly and if the reasons for them are clear.

Developing effective means of disciplining young people who have sexually abused is especially important. It might be a parent's automatic response to threaten the child given the seriousness of the behaviour. However, if you respond in a physically aggressive or verbally abusive way there is a danger that your child may withdraw and that you will lose your child's confidence in you as someone to go to in times of trouble, as the following example shows:

> Sean was a 16-year-old young man who was accused of sexually assaulting a 12-year-old boy. Sean's father said that he would 'kill' him if he found out that it was true that he had sexually abused. As his father had a history of physical abuse of Sean's mother, this blocked all work being offered to Sean, who even two years later was too scared to own up to his behaviour.

5. Setting boundaries for your children and helping them to develop appropriate ways of behaving

As indicated above I believe that physical punishment is a poor way of disciplining children and it can, ironically, lead to further conflict in the relationship between parent and child, and more problematic behaviour from the child. Whether or not to use physical punishment is a parent's personal choice, but physical abuse or assault of a child is against the law. There is an increasing emphasis being placed by experts on avoiding ways of disciplining children that are based on retaliation (e.g. hitting or humiliating a child) and instead trying to give the child an opportunity to put things right. In particular, physically punishing a young person who has sexually abused is likely to reinforce and promote some of the kinds of distorted thoughts that can lead to sexual abuse in the first place, e.g. 'It's OK to control people by hurting them', 'I am not loved, nobody cares for me' or 'Someone is going to pay for this'.

Alternatives to physical punishment
There are other ways to try to enforce discipline and to deal with a negative behaviour without having to resort to physical means. One idea is to give out a negative consequence which is connected to the seriousness of the behaviour. So, for example, a child who damages property could have pocket money deducted until he can pay for the damage caused. Alternatively, you can take away a reward or privilege, e.g. grounding or stopping the child watching TV. The key to success in both cases is to be consistent. This means both in *how* and *when* you use discipline. The measures you take should be logical. If a child will not do his bit in tidying up the house, then not being able to enjoy the benefits of a tidy house,

for example watching TV, is a logical consequence. You should also let your child know why you have decided on a particular disciplinary measure and you should, whatever else you do, follow through with what you say will happen. This gives children clear messages about the consequences of their actions. If they want to avoid the negative consequence they can do this by avoiding the behaviour. This is the best way of shaping a child's behaviour in the long-term. Whatever methods you choose, children learn and develop their conscience about their actions best when parents use reasoning as a way of discipline and do so in a warm way.

Discouraging negative behaviours
It is now recognised that, just as parents can affect the ways their children behave, so children in turn can affect their parents' behaviour (Maccoby, 2000; Strand, 2000). If a child behaves badly and a parent gives in to the behaviour, the child may well stop behaving badly and the way you have responded has been 'reinforced'. For example, parents commonly will back down after a child has behaved badly. For example, a child who screams for chocolate in the supermarket and embarrasses a parent may get the chocolate and may stop screaming. In this way both the parent and the child are rewarded (the child who gets the chocolate and the parent who gets some quiet). The trouble is that although the immediate problem is solved, the parent pays the price for this in the longer-term, as it is likely that the child will develop further difficult and, increasingly aggressive behaviours to get its own way. This is just one example of how we can unwittingly behave as parents to further encourage or 'reinforce' our children's problematic behaviours.

If you feel that this is something that has happened in your family, the following techniques may be helpful to deal with your children in a way which encourages them to replace the negative behaviours with positive ones:

- Do not respond to a child's negative behaviour with positive attention. This means that the child will feel rewarded and the behaviour is likely to become a way for the child of gaining this kind of attention again.

- Reward your child's neutral or OK behaviours, not just those that are particularly positive or good. Studies (Strand, 2000) have shown that the more positive attention you give your children and the more positive interactions you have with them, the more likely it is that they will listen to you and do what you ask when they misbehave.

- Ignore the negative behaviour altogether, hoping that the child will stop behaving that way. Children have sometimes learnt that they can get attention through behaving badly. By not responding you take away the child's motivation for behaving in this way. If you are considering trying this you need to think carefully about the kinds of behaviours it is appropriate to ignore. It is not appropriate to ignore any behaviour that puts the child at risk or places any other person in danger, including sexually abusive behaviour.

Again, **consistency** (in how you behave) and **predictability** (in what your children understand will happen if they misbehave) is the most important thing.

Ways to teach children acceptable behaviour
Part of the process of helping your child to have an abuse-free future is to help him to develop a sense of acceptable behaviour in non-sexual aspects of his life. If there are new rules introduced about sexual behaviours and yet the rules about how to treat people with respect in other situations contradict these, then the messages you are trying to give your child can be undermined. Consistency is the key; in other words, not responding to the same behaviour one way, one day, and another way, the next. This can be difficult as our own moods and problems, as parents, can get in the way of us thinking clearly and responding

calmly to our children. However, the following are some ideas that can be applied across different situations in order to help teach children what acceptable behaviours are:

- Praise your child's good behaviour, even if it is relatively minor or seems overshadowed by other negative behaviours. Show your children that you are pleased with them for what they do right, rather than always focusing on what they do wrong.

- Start more conversations with your child. Children with behaviour problems are less likely to have been approached by their parents for conversations.

- Treat your child with respect and dignity, the way you would want to be treated yourself. Sexually abusive behaviour can strip the child of his self belief and dignity, but demonstrating to your child that he is still loved and that you are interested in him can raise the child's level of self respect.

- Tell your child directly and clearly what you expect. Don't assume that your child knows how you want him to behave in any given situation.

- Think about your environment and how it might support negative behaviours. Change it to encourage the kind of behaviours you expect from your child. Remove the kind of things that might trigger the negative behaviours. For instance, if you are concerned about your child's aggression, make sure that there are no videos around which support or glorify aggression; if your child is withdrawn and bored, try to think about activities to interest the child, and so on.

- Encourage a sense of predictability and routine. Let your child know about changes and plans and when they will happen. On a day-to-day basis, discuss plans and structure with your child.

- Offer appropriate choices to your child and be prepared to allow your child to follow through with the choice, for example, 'you can spend your money how you like but once it is gone there won't be any left'. Allowing children to experience the consequences of their actions safely is a key way that children and young people learn. Clearly, you need to make some judgements about what kind of choices and consequences are safe and appropriate for a young person who has sexually abused.

- Model the kind of behaviour you would like back from your child. For example, if you want to encourage sharing or responsibility, show how to do this through your own ways of responding to your child.

6. Having fun times with your child

An important general goal of parenting is to have fun and share enjoyment of activities and situations with your children. By sharing such positive experiences you can develop closeness and warmth in your relationship. This poses a challenge to a parent of a child who has sexually abused, as such opportunities may be very limited. You might simply not want to invest this kind of time in your child, especially when you are feeling angry. Many parents tell me that there is little opportunity for fun following abuse in their families. However, having enjoyable or positive times, ones that are safe and appropriate to the child and others, is an important way of repairing the damage done to your parent-child relationship. Such experiences can help strengthen the bond between you and your child and can make it more likely that your child will come to you for help in the future. Making a list of positive and enjoyable things you can do with your child is a good way to begin (see Exercise 18).

Fathers and mothers

Most of this book has talked about 'parents' without drawing out the distinctions between mothers and fathers. This is a deliberate decision I took in order to make the book relevant to both male and female carers, single carers and carers who are in same-sex relationships. Families come in very many different forms and parents, if indeed there are two carers in a family, may work out their roles in different ways between each other. Sometimes, parents fall into particular roles and assume that certain things are their 'job' or responsibility, simply because of their gender. For example, women are more likely to take on the caring role in families and men take more of a back seat in things such as housework and looking after the children. This is not because women are naturally better at this, but sometimes because we assume that this is what we should do. We very often base our own parenting on what we have learnt from our own parents; how our own mothers and fathers behaved towards each other and towards us as children. There are many reasons why we might need to look again at this and make some changes, especially after a child has sexually abused.

Firstly, what was considered normal in families is changing quickly now. For example, in 1971, only seven per cent of families with children were lone mother families; by 1998–99 this had more than trebled to twenty-two per cent. Lone fathers caring for children now account for two per cent of families. Only seventy-five per cent of families now have a married or living-together couple, as opposed to ninety-two per cent in 1971 (General Household Survey, 2000). Even in households where there are two parents, more women work out of the house now and some men are realising that it is not fair to leave all the caring work to women. Therefore, the things we learnt from our own parents about what a mother or father should do may not be appropriate today.

Secondly, the impact of a child sexually abusing means that it is essential, where a mother and father share the care of children, to think about how the two people concerned can support each other and help each other, even if this means doing things which either one had not considered to be his or her job previously. This does not necessarily mean doing the same things, but it means fairness between parents and equal value for the different roles each takes on.

The following sections highlight some of the particular points for mothers, and for fathers, when a young person has sexually abused.

Being a mother

Many of the mothers who have come together in the parents' group at the Kaleidoscope project have gained strength from other mothers and have realised that their feelings are not unique but are shared by other women. There have been expressions of pain and failure which are acutely felt by mothers who may have been the one person in the family who has cared for the child from birth. As mothers usually take on most of the caring role in the family, many women have talked of how they feel like a bad mother. This can be especially the case if the abuse happened in your house when you were there ('How did I not see what was going on') and if another of your children was the victim ('I failed to protect my child'). Most painful of all can be the feeling that you are responsible for the sexual behaviours ('Where did I go wrong?')

Mothers may be particularly vulnerable as they are usually the one who is at home for more of the time when there are two parents and they usually take on much of the monitoring of risk situations in the family after the abuse is discovered. This can weigh very heavily. Where there are two carers in a family, mothers should not have to take this burden onto their own shoulders alone. Fathers in families should be prepared to share the burden and to take on a fuller role in the care of the children. Mothers often receive all or most attention from professionals after abuse, whilst fathers are overlooked. At the same time, the presence of a mother who has not abused children in cases of sexual abuse can make all the difference to outcomes for children.

Being a father

Facing up to the emotions that you feel as a father following your child's abusive behaviour can be difficult for men. Many men have been brought up to hide their feelings or to believe that showing emotion is a sign of weakness. This is absolutely not true but it is difficult to get away from if this is the message you were given as a child. Some men have such difficulty with coping with the strength of the feelings they have inside that this comes out as anger, aggression or even violence in some cases. Some fathers feel guilty, particularly when a young man has abused, because they realise that they have encouraged aggression or violence, or given their children a poor example of how a man should behave.

Although not true in all cases, in my experience fathers have been more likely to try to explain away their child's abusive behaviour as 'horseplay' and to dismiss the possibility of it occurring again, perhaps because the reality of facing up to the abuse is so frightening to them. Learning about your child's sexually problematic behaviour (e.g. about consent and power) may make you realise that there are changes you need to make to the way you express your sexuality or about how you use your power.

Some fathers I have worked with have felt that professionals have assumed that the child who has sexually abused must also be a victim of abuse and that suspicion has automatically fallen on them as the father. Other fathers have talked to me about how the sexual abuse has made them confused about the kind of relationship they should have with their children. They can feel less able to take part in activities where there is intimacy with their children, for example they can be frightened of bathing or putting their children to bed as they fear that this might be misinterpreted or seen as abusive. Ironically for these men, the sexual abuse takes them further away from reaping some of the positive benefits of being a parent and sharing intimate moments with their child.

Many of the studies of fathers' involvement in cases where children have been abused repeatedly point out how 'invisible' fathers are (Trotter, 1998). Sometimes professionals assume that the responsibility for looking after and protecting the children falls on the mother in the family and therefore they ask little of men, who might actually be able to offer a great deal to their female partners and to their children. Sometimes fathers can contribute to this by their unwillingness to become involved, leaving attendance at meetings to the mother in the household, or by being silent in meetings, etc. Such withdrawal, either on purpose or unintentionally, from the difficult issues to be faced is likely to mean that the young person who has been abused gets the message that their father is not concerned. The key is to make yourself take part even if this feels like it is difficult or upsetting. You might also like to:

- Review your role in the house and look carefully, and talk carefully, about what else you could do to share the care of your children.

- Ensure that you are participating as fully as you can in making your family safe and in any professional work being offered.

- Learn how to express your feelings in a healthy way.

- Be aware that you have a crucial role to play in showing your child how a male should behave.

- Take this opportunity to review all the assumptions you made in the past about what it is to be male and try to correct any unhealthy attitudes or behaviours you may carry from your past.

Summary points from this section

- Use the opportunity created by the abuse to review your parenting styles and the roles you have in your family.
- Consistency is a key aspect in effective parenting.
- Physical punishment should be avoided and other constructive ways developed to encourage positive behaviours.
- Spending 'quality' time with your children, giving them opportunities to succeed and develop self esteem are essential parts of positive parenting.

Questions to consider

- What opportunities can you create to spend safe and positive time with your children, despite the issues created by the sexual abuse?
- Are there aspects of your parenting that you need to amend?
- If there are two parents in your family, are roles and jobs divided fairly? How can you ensure that each person is supported as best as possible?

Exercise 15: Sources of conflict with your child

Purpose. This exercise is designed to help you to learn about sources of conflict with your child and to consider how best to deal with this.

1. The following list represents the kinds of common situations in families that can typically lead to conflict between parents and children. Look through the list and tick in the boxes according to how often each applies in your case. The empty boxes at the bottom of the list are for any additional sources of conflict with your child that you wish to add.

Potential source of conflict	Often	Some-times	Hardly ever	Never
Watching television				
Bed times				
Bath times				
Mornings				
Helping out around the house				
Child going out				
Arguments or fighting between brothers or sisters				
Child's untidiness				
Child's friends				
Money issues				
Sexual issues				
Additional sources of conflict:				

2. For each item you have marked 'often' write down how such conflicts build up, as follows:

2.1 How often does it happen? (every day, every week, etc.)

....

....

....

....

2.2 What happens exactly?

....

....

....

....

2.3 How does the conflict end at the moment?

....

....

....

....

2.4 How could the conflict situation be handled better?

....

....

....

....

Exercise 16: Dealing with your child's difficult or challenging behaviours

Purpose. This exercise is designed to help you think about your responses to difficult or challenging behaviours that might be demonstrated by your child or children. These may be totally unconnected to the sexually abusive behaviour (see the next section in this chapter on how to deal with difficult situations connected to the abuse) but these are the kind of behaviours that can be so wearing that they undermine your ability to respond positively to your child. They may also follow a pattern and trying to see the links between behaviours and how you respond can be helpful.

1. Think about the non-sexual behaviours that your child displays that are difficult for you. For each, write down:

1.1 What happens?

....

....

1.2 Where does it happen?

....

....

1.3 Who is involved?

....

....

1.4 When does the problem seem to happen?

....

....

1.5 What happens just before?

....

....

1.6 What happens afterwards?

....

....

1.7 How could you respond better to the problem?

....

....

1.8 What could you do to stop the problem or prevent the problem happening?

....

....

Exercise 17: Reviewing your parenting style and method

Purpose. This exercise is designed to help you to consider your style of parenting and the methods you use.

Think back to the relationship you have had as a parent with your children. Reflect on what you have done well, and not so well, as a parent and then answer the following questions:

1. Consistency

1.1 How consistent am I with my child? Mark with a cross on the line:

Always consistent	Usually respond consistently	Often changeable	Totally changeable

1.2 Ways in which my parenting can be inconsistent:

....

....

....

....

1.3 What I need to do to be more consistent with my child:

....

....

....

....

2. Firmness and fairness

2.1 How often do I demand good behaviour from my child and respond firmly when they do something wrong? Mark with a cross on the line:

Always give in	Sometimes give in	Usually respond firmly	Always respond firmly

2.2 Ways in which my parenting can be unfair:

....

....

....

....

2.3 What I need to do to be firm and fair with my children:

....

....

....

....

3. Responsiveness and taking an interest

3.1 How responsive am I to my child?

| Always take an interest | Sometimes take an interest | Often can't face my child | Always avoid my child |

●──●

3.2 Ways in which my parenting can be unresponsive:

....

....

....

....

3.3 What I need to do to respond to my children and their needs better:

....

....

....

....

Exercise 18: Spending time with your child

Purpose. This exercise is designed to help you to think about how you can spend positive time with your child in order to improve your relationship.

As a parent of a young person who has abused, you need to think carefully about the potential risks involved with any activity you plan with your child. It is important to be confident that you can do things with your child, whilst at the same time separate out things that are unwise and unsafe given your situation.

1. In the left hand column make a list of activities to avoid or to encourage. Once you have done this, in the middle column rate the activities according to the risks it could present (to other children, to you or to your child). In the third column write down what the benefits or drawbacks would be, and to whom.

Activities/ Situations to avoid	Risk rating (1–10)	Possible drawbacks (and why):
Activities/ Situations to encourage	Risk rating (1–10)	Possible benefits (and to whom):

Developing New Ways of Dealing with Risk Situations

Monitoring and managing risk

A **risk situation** is a situation that could put your child back on the pathway towards sexually abusive behaviour. The idea behind the emphasis on risk is that by *avoiding* or *dealing with* the kind of conditions that accompanied the abuse in the first place, we can make it less likely that the abuse will occur again. Accepting that there are situations which involve some risk and therefore should be avoided is sensible, the mark of a concerned and committed parent. This does not mean that you think your child will abuse again, merely that you are concerned enough to realise that he needs to avoid putting himself in certain positions, or indeed avoid being put in such situations by other people.

Risk management is a term used by professionals to refer to the need to have ways of dealing with risk situations that will occur on a day-to-day basis at home and in the community. Being confident enough to tackle these potential risk situations before they become a problem or end up in abusive behaviour, is the essence of effective risk management. Risk management involves parents taking some responsibility for monitoring situations which could lead to abuse. This means being alert, watching for signs that everything is not right, and stopping situations that might possibly lead the child to start to think about abusing again. Much of monitoring, or risk management, are the common sense steps that concerned parents would want to take following abuse in their family. Sensible precautions are necessary, but it is important to keep this in balance, as becoming obsessed to the point that you and your family cannot live your life is not the best way of managing risk.

Sometimes, parents find it hard to strike this balance, as can be seen in the two following examples:

- **Mary** was a mother whose fourteen-year-old son had abused her ten-year-old daughter. Mary had to monitor risks in the household when her son returned home after six months living with his grandparents. Mary felt that she could not allow her son to be in the same room as her daughter when she was not there. This became so extreme that she insisted that her son left the room and stood outside the bathroom whilst she went to the toilet. Her daughter was made to sleep on a mattress in her mother's bedroom at night, but even so, Mary would lie awake at night listening and worrying about what might happen were she to go straight to sleep.

- **Steve**'s fifteen-year-old daughter had abused her younger sisters, aged five and seven. After some work was carried out with the daughter, she returned home. The younger sisters were pleased as they had missed their older sister. Steve wanted the family to be 'normal' again and didn't want his daughter to feel that she was no longer trusted. Whilst he stopped her babysitting (which was the situation in which the abuse had first started) he didn't stop the three children playing together for long periods upstairs in a bedroom whilst he was downstairs. The abuse continued.

The balance between sensible monitoring and taking appropriate precautions can be a difficult one. If Mary's son was so dangerous that he could not be trusted to be alone with his sister for one minute, then he should not have been allowed to return to live with her. At the same time, it was unwise for Steve to allow his daughter to have the kind of unsupervised contact she was able to have with her sisters.

The following section offers some detailed guidance on how you can manage risk, and monitor situations effectively, in order to avoid the mistakes that both Steve and Mary made.

Managing risk in the family

Whether your child is living with you full-time or occasionally comes to visit your home, it is important to consider how you can manage any risk situations that he may present in the home. The kinds of risk situations important in your family will be specific to your situation, depending on:

- The nature of the abuse that took place.
- The needs and vulnerabilities of the victims (if they are living in the house).
- The physical layout within your home and the challenges presented by this.
- The stage of the work that your child has reached and his level of awareness.
- Your child's ability to contribute to the management of risk.

It is a good idea to look again at the factors which contributed to your child's sexually abusive behaviour as these may highlight particular areas for you to be especially mindful of. You should consider both:

1. Things you can **do** to help reduce risk; and
2. Things you should **avoid** to help reduce risk situations.

1. Things you can **do** to help reduce risk

1.1 Try to create a 'culture of openness' in your family

By this I mean a family environment, where your children are free to talk about any problems or worries they have. Taking an interest in your children's daily activities, school for example, tells them that you are interested in them and lays down the foundation for your child to be able to let you know if things are not going well. If you are not used to having this kind of relationship with your children, then you cannot expect them to begin to open up to you in this way immediately, and you will need to aim for gradual change. One way of encouraging this is to set aside time each day to talk with your children about what they have done that day. If you can fit this into an activity that your child likes or into a routine where your child has your attention then you might find that you can build up this kind of culture of openness and that your child slowly begins to open up about his worries. It is worth stressing here that this will not only help children in your family who may be vulnerable, but it can be a crucial avenue for the child who has abused to talk about feelings and worries. In this way, you will be providing your child with an opportunity to deal with problematic feelings or distorted thoughts before they become translated into abusive behaviours.

1.2 Ensure that all your children have appropriate sex education

This includes vulnerable children, as well as the child who has abused. Do not assume that because your child has been engaging in sexual behaviours he has all the sexual knowledge he needs. Many young people who abuse have limited information about sex or, indeed, have many distorted ideas about sex that need correcting if abuse is to be avoided in the future. Sometimes these distorted ideas have been communicated to other children in the family, even if these children have not themselves been abused. Creating a healthy balance in your family about sexual matters will help this. Resist the temptation of 'squashing' any open sexual discussion or appropriate sexual behaviours in your family as this is more likely to drive sexual behaviours into secrecy.

2. Things to **avoid** in the home

The following points may be helpful as a general guide to how you can manage risk situations in your home (Pithers, Gray, Cunningham and Lane, 1993). You should check them out with any professionals involved with your family over the sexual abuse, as these may have particular information or may wish to offer specific advice or ideas.

2.1 Take away the opportunities your child has to abuse within your home

Taking away opportunities that your child might have to abuse again or which encourages him to abuse again, is a sensible and vital step. Think about a person who had an alcohol problem who has been 'dry', or not drinking, for some time. You would not want to tempt fate by leaving open bottles in front of him or her. It would be sensible to make sure that alcohol did not come into the household. This is similar for young people who have sexually abused. Trying to cut down on opportunities that might 'tempt' the child to abuse again is therefore in your child's best interests. You should not worry about this being a sign that you do not trust your child, or that you do not believe any assurances he has given about not abusing again. In particular, you should:

- Make sure you do not leave the child who has abused with vulnerable children, especially if they are around the age of known victims. Many parents tie themselves up in knots about this, but you need to be sensible about it. For example, if you are in the house with the young person who has abused and a younger sibling, you cannot keep your eyes on both children all the time. However, allowing the two children to play in a bedroom with the door shut and with no supervision is clearly a bad idea. Use your common sense and your knowledge of your child's previous abusive behaviour to judge how far you have to go on this. Seek advice from a professional if you are unsure. Encourage the young person to exercise some responsibility about this, agreeing the situations he needs to avoid. It should not just be down to you.

- Make sure that your child does not use the bathroom at the same time as other children *even when you are there* to supervise. Even if you are there to stop anything untoward or harmful happening, it is not a good idea for your child to see younger children without clothes on, or in other vulnerable positions. With planning and routine, (e.g. before bathing a younger child, checking whether the young person needs the toilet and other such common-sense strategies) there should be no need for the young person to have to go into the bathroom at the same time as a vulnerable child. All children in the family should be confident in their ability to get privacy about their own bodies. The young person who has abused should also not be allowed to enter siblings' bedrooms without an adult being there. Measures should also be taken about nudity in the house too, as are appropriate to the ages of children in the house. For example, it is common for toddlers to run about without clothes, but this is not acceptable behaviour for teenagers.

- If your child is playing with a child who is not seen as vulnerable (e.g. perhaps a school friend of the same age or an older sibling) you should still check on them regularly.

- Stop your children playing any games which the young person who has abused might have used to get another child to go along with the abuse or that the young person might experience in a sexual way. Examples are tickling games, hide and seek, aggressive games or games that involve hurting or secrets, and games that involve children's bodies such as playing doctors and nurses. The young person should be told that such games are not appropriate any more, that he should take on responsibility for not initiating these games, and for not responding or saying 'yes' if invited by a younger child or children. Sometimes, a vulnerable child might attempt to start one of these games, as this is how they have been expected to behave in the past. The young person needs to know what to say and how to gently refuse to take part in them any more. It is advisable to help the young person to think about what to say in such situations before they happen.

2.2 Cut back on experiences that might increase a young person's problematic or inappropriate sexual thoughts

Here you are cutting down on situations that might encourage the young person to think about abusive sex or begin to justify it in their mind:

- Try not to let the young person see scenes of violent or abusive sexuality on TV, film, the Internet, etc. It is virtually impossible to stop your child seeing all sexual images: you need not prevent the low-key and generally normal sexual imagery any child might see on a music video or a soap opera. However, anything of an explicit or aggressive nature should be avoided. Think carefully about whether you should take away the TV or computer from the young person's bedroom, especially if he has satellite or cable TV or Internet connection. Do not have pornographic magazines or images around the house. Even if you put them away somewhere, your child is likely to find them. See the guidelines later in this chapter for more details on dealing with sex on TV and the Internet.

- If the young person or anyone else who comes into your home uses sexual language, jokes, stories or behaviours, try to stop this by explaining why it is not appropriate and how it can have a damaging effect upon other people.

- Make sure that when adults in the house do sexual things, they do so in complete privacy and cannot be heard or seen by the young person or other children.

- Encourage the young person's healthy sexual expression, for example that it is OK to masturbate in private as long as the young person is not having abusive thoughts at the same time, and talk openly to your children about sex and sexual knowledge. If you can manage this, they are more likely to grow up knowing that non-abusive sex is not a dirty or secretive thing, but a normal and pleasurable part of people's lives. Look at the guidelines and exercises in Chapter 6 for more details about how to talk about sex to the young person who has abused.

2.3 Stop and correct any examples of misuse of power

Chapters 1 and 3 showed that sexually abusive behaviour is when a person uses his power in a way to hurt others. It is really important to help your child learn ways to handle difficulties or problems, or simply to face other people, in a way which does not involve them misusing his power, for example:

- If you see your child using his power (the power that may come from his age, physical strength, intelligence, gender, etc.) in any way to hurt or control others you should step in and stop this. Most times such incidents will not be sexual in nature, but the danger is that the young person will continue to think that it is OK to use power or force to get his own way. Instead, your child should be taught to solve problems in other ways. You can emphasise concepts such as being patient, sharing, taking turns, talking things through with the other person or reaching an agreement. Of course, you will be much more effective in this if you yourself show these qualities to your children in your own behaviour.

- Help your child deal with feelings of anger. If he is quick to get worked up or angry when with other people, or when not getting his own way, try to encourage your child to take time out and to calm down.

2.4 Correct any distorted thoughts that you notice in your child

In Chapter 3 we saw how young people can develop distorted or faulty thoughts that can provide the foundations for abusive behaviour. Even if your child is making good progress with work to encourage him not to abuse in the future, there may be times when he slips back into distorted thinking, particularly when under pressure or stressed. Correcting these distorted thoughts calmly but immediately whenever you see them creeping back is one way of helping your child stay away from pathways which could lead him back towards abusive behaviour:

- If you hear your child say something that could support sexually abusive behaviour you should correct this. For example, a young person who says 'all girls are slags' may be implying that young women are fair game for sex and have no right to say 'no' to a male. It is important to correct statements such as these, for example by saying something like 'the word slag is horrible and disrespectful to young women. Many young women choose not to have sex and that's fine. Others do have sex and should be able to choose to have sex as long as they are in control'.

- If your child says something that suggests he is thinking of himself as a victim, perhaps in response to some form of monitoring that you have put into place, then it is important to correct these statements. Again, young people who are feeling sorry for themselves unduly may be close to rejoining a pathway to abusive behaviour by finding ways to make themselves feel better. For example, 'It's not fair that you always make my life miserable by telling me what I can and can't do' can be corrected by 'There are things that you can't do now because of the abuse and it would not be fair to you or to other children if I let you put yourself in a dangerous situation again.'

2.5 Stay calm and relaxed if you can

This is easier said than done, of course. Many parents have talked to me about how uptight and stressed they feel trying to keep things safe in their homes. Feeling so stressed actually means that you are less effective in monitoring risk situations because you are less likely to notice clues from your children if you are tense and tired. Children can pick up on their parents' tension and can become worried and upset by this. Although this may be difficult, if you can keep relatively calm and relaxed, but at the same time actually **do** and **avoid** the things I suggest above, then this can make the whole family environment safer and more enjoyable.

Specific risk situations to watch out for

Aside from the 'dos' and 'don'ts' above, there are some specific issues which are so commonly associated with the behaviour of a young person who may be at risk of abusing again, that you should be highly sensitive to these and pick up on them immediately. If you notice any of the following signs, you will need to face your child with what you have seen and encourage him to talk about what is happening:

- Any sudden or gradual changes in your child's behaviour or moods.
- Situations when your child seems to be withdrawing or putting himself in an isolated position.
- Times when your child disappears for long periods in the home or outside the house.
- Aggressive play or tickling games amongst siblings.
- Physical contact of all kinds between the young person who has abused and vulnerable people (children and adults).
- Any situation where the child appears to be taking anger out on others, especially those who are vulnerable.

Dealing with sexual imagery or programmes about abuse on TV

Parents have repeatedly talked about the embarrassment and confusion they feel if they are in a situation with the young person who has abused and something of a sexual nature, or even a discussion about paedophiles, or such like, comes on television. It is important to have proper ways of dealing with these issues, so that you and your children do not feel embarrassed or uncomfortable, as is reported by this mother:

> *We would all sit there together going redder and redder, nobody daring to say anything but everybody knowing what everyone was thinking about.*

> (Mother of a 15-year-old who had abused boys in the neighbourhood talking about sex scenes on TV)

If the programme which is embarrassing is a discussion about sex offenders or paedophiles, you may wish to stress to your child some positives about how he has been addressing his problems, emphasising that you know that there are good things about him. Many TV programmes on this matter are focused on adult sex offenders and can be quite hostile in their approach to people who have sexually abused. As a rule, you should try to ensure that your child is not left feeling 'different' or bad about what has been said. You could use this as an opportunity to check how your child is feeling about any work that is going on or about how they are coping. It is, of course, important to avoid doing this in the presence of the victim or other vulnerable children.

Computers, the Internet and pornography

The use of computers and the Internet has now become an ordinary part of many people's lives. It is an area where parents can find that their children have more knowledge, understanding and skills than they have. Some parents rely on their teenage children to sort out computer problems and to get 'on-line' in the first place. The Internet enables people from all over the world to get access to information on any subject imaginable in a matter of seconds. Whilst there are many benefits in this, there are also some drawbacks that parents in general, and especially parents whose children have a sexual behaviour problem, need to be aware of.

In particular, there is an enormous amount of pornography on the Internet and young people can find it easily. This includes very explicit pictures and video clips of highly explicit or 'hardcore' sexual acts. Clearly, this is material that it is important to protect all children from, but it can be particularly damaging for young people who have sexually abused to see such pornographic material. This is for several reasons.

Firstly, pornography in general, and especially 'hardcore' pornography on the Internet, encourages the development or 'growth' of ideas about sex which are very close to those that a person committing sexual offences may have in his head. Pornography tends to show females as always willing to do what males want sexually and as always sexually available for males. Sometimes, the pictures and words used even suggest that women like to be raped or hurt by a man sexually. Young people may very easily take ideas from seeing such pictures such as 'I should be able to get sex from a female whenever I want it' or 'it's OK for me to hurt a female in sex' or 'it doesn't matter what the female wants or says'.

Secondly, and even more dangerous as far as people who have sexually abused are concerned, child pornography is available on the Internet. Even where the females shown having sex are adults, they can be dressed up as if they were children and shown having sex with much older men. Again, for someone who has sexually abused and who might have been working hard to stop sexually abusing, seeing these images would be very damaging indeed.

Thirdly, there are groups of paedophiles who organise themselves on the Internet and set out to draw children into their groups by using chat rooms, etc.

As a parent, it is therefore important that you make sure that you know how to keep your child safe on the Internet. I work with a growing number of young people who say that their motivation to abuse came from looking at pornography on the Internet, for example:

> Mike was a fifteen-year-old young man who lived with his mother and father and eight-year-old sister. He was successful at school and had a happy home life. He was very skilled in using the computer and Internet and began looking at pornography. He became addicted to seeing pornography on the Internet and seemed to spend less and less time with his friends out of the house. It was as if the Internet became his world and he was happy to cut himself off from all those around him. The pictures made him highly sexually aroused for most of the time when he was at home and he began to force his sister to do the things he had seen on the computer and imagined himself doing. Mike could not stop himself from looking at the pornography, nor could he stop himself from acting out with his sister the fantasies these pictures gave him.

As can be seen from the example of Mike, a child or teenager's excessive use of the Internet, especially late at night, may be a clue that there is a potential problem. Mike's use of the Internet in his abuse of his sister meant that it was just too risky to allow him to use the Internet after the abuse was discovered and this facility had to be taken away from him. However, it is not always necessary to take such drastic action for all young people, especially as learning about computers and new technologies is an important educational goal. Here are some ideas about the kind of sensible precautions you should take for the safe use of the Internet in your family:

- Place the computer in a shared or public room in your home (e.g. a living room) rather than allowing a young person who has sexually abused to have it in his bedroom.

- Get to know the Internet Service Provider (often referred to as ISPs) that your child uses. Ask your child to show you how to log on, if you do not know. Many ISPs offer parents help to stop children accessing offensive and adult material. Use an Internet 'blocking or filtering' programme. Tell your child that you are doing this and will be checking to see what has been visited from time to time. These programmes are not foolproof, nor are they a replacement for a common sense approach. If you don't know what parental internet control tools are, or how they work, find out. Try: http://childdevelopmentinfo.com/health_safety/bair.htm

- Establish rules for Internet usage with your children. These should include the maximum amounts of time they can spend on-line, a 'no pornography' rule, etc. You will need to be reasonable and set appropriate expectations. Try to understand and balance your child's needs, interests and natural curiosity as a teenager, with his needs as a young person who has sexually abused.

- Sometimes, sit with your child whilst he uses the computer and, occasionally ask your child to show you the websites he visits, and his list of website 'bookmarks' or 'favourites'. As with other problems your child might have, encourage your child to tell you if they have a problem or concern about the Internet.

- Make sure that your child does not give out personal information without your permission. This includes e-mail address, home address, school name or telephone number. It is especially important that children and young people do not give out this information in a public message such as in a chatroom or a bulletin board.

- Never allow your child to meet in person someone they have met on-line through a chat room. Make sure your child is aware that people on-line may not be who they seem. Because you cannot see the person, it is easy for someone to misrepresent himself. So, someone claiming to be a fifteen-year-old young woman might actually be a fifty-year-old man.

If some of the above points make little sense to you because you are not used to using a computer, try to get the advice of someone who is.

What should I tell other children in my family who weren't abused about what has happened?

Parents often feel a dilemma about what information to give to other children in the family who were not sexually abused by the young person. Questions such as 'Should I tell at all?', 'When should I tell', 'How much should I say?' and 'How shall I say it?' are most common.

There are no clear-cut answers to these questions and the dealing with these issues will depend upon many things, such as how old the children concerned are, the nature of the abuse that has taken place and whether the young person who has abused has remained in the home. Saying nothing might appear the easiest thing but is often the least satisfactory option. At the same time, you may be right not to want to give other children too much information that would be in itself inappropriate or harmful.

The following points should help in facing these dilemmas:

- Young children do not need to know the sexual detail of what has happened. But they might need to know some key messages about self-protection and what to do were any kind of approach made to them. This is where it is doubly important for you as a parent to know how the young person went about the abuse in the past, so that you can be alert to the signs and so that you can give siblings specific advice. For example, if you know that the young person abused his victim by trying to get her to play a 'special game', you could make the sibling aware that such games are not OK. Whilst you quite rightly may not want to give your children too much information, it is important that they have enough information both to make sense of their situation and also to be protected. As a basic principle, siblings have a right to be informed about issues that directly affect them. For example, an older brother or sister disappearing from the home without a clear explanation as to why, is likely to leave the younger child confused and could be damaging.

- You should also consider what might happen if you do not tell the child yourself and how this might place the child in difficulties in other situations. For example, it is best that non-abused siblings find out from you, as their parent, in a balanced and planned way, rather than through rumours at school or comments in the local community. Unfortunately, sometimes younger siblings of young people who have abused are called names or made fun of by other children. By giving some basic information about what the problem is and how to cope with such comments you can help prepare your child should such comments or teasing occur.

- Additionally, if the young person who has abused is aware that his non-abused siblings have been given some basic information about what has happened and that they know what to do to get help, this can be a good way of making it less likely that he will try to draw them into the abuse.

Two final points on this issue are vital. Firstly, younger siblings need to be helped to deal with the information once they have it. It is not appropriate, for example, to give a child information about the abuse one minute and the next to threaten the child with severe consequences if she passes this on. Secondly, remember more than anything that sexual abuse is an abuse of power and relies on secrecy. Younger siblings are very often vulnerable given their age. Secrecy in the family about the major issues that are affecting your lives will not help.

Helping other children in your family develop protection skills

You can help your children develop ways of responding to protect themselves in a situation where they may be at risk of abuse. These simple messages are important for all children, regardless of sexual abuse by a sibling in a family, but having these skills is clearly important in situations where a child's sibling has sexually abused. Even if you think that it is unlikely that your child would abuse his sibling, it is worth giving these messages to all of your children. Don't assume that your child will automatically tell you about any abuse. Children often do not tell about sexual abuse by their siblings. This is for a variety of reasons, including the use of threats and force by the abuser, the fact that the abuser is a powerful person in their lives, or sometimes because the child does not realise that the abuse is wrong.

It is important to let young children know about the 'private' parts of their bodies, including genitals, bottom, mouth. They should be taught that it is not OK for other people to touch them there or to ask them to touch the other person's private parts. The child should be taught that any touch where the other person tells the child to keep the touch a secret is a 'bad touch'. If you can give these messages to children from an early age (i.e. from being toddlers) they are more likely to grow up confident about their own bodies and their abilities to have control over who does what to their bodies.

Sometimes parents are worried about giving their child too much sex education too early. Whilst it is important to be sensitive to the age of your child, it is also important not to leave it too late. As a rule, follow the guidelines below, also paying attention to the section on normal sexual development in Chapter 1:

- Up to three years: Teach your child the proper names for body parts.
- Two to five years: Teach your child about private parts of the body and how to say no to sexual advances. Give straightforward answers about sex.
- Six to nine years: Discuss safety away from home and the difference between good touch and bad touch. Encourage your child to ask questions.
- Ten to thirteen years: Stress personal safety. Start to discuss OK sexual behaviours.
- Thirteen to eighteen years: Continue to stress personal safety. Discuss rape, (including 'date rape', i.e. being raped by a boyfriend), sexually transmitted diseases, and pregnancy.

Four simple messages from you will help your children to understand that they can say 'no' to situations that make them feel uncomfortable. These are suitable for even very young children:

1. Say 'No' or 'Stop it' in a loud voice.
2. Get out of the situation and find somewhere which is safe.
3. Tell you or another trusted adult, e.g. other family member, social worker, teacher, etc., what has happened.
4. Let your children know that you would believe them and that they would not get into trouble.

It is important to remember that developing your child's self-protection skills is not, in itself, a replacement for dealing with risk issues. As we have seen above, the most important two things you can do to make sure that your children are safe in your family is to **monitor risk situations** and to **encourage more open communication** in your family about all things, but especially about feelings and problems. In a family situation following abuse, the emotions that everyone has to cope with are so strong that sometimes individuals withdraw into themselves and parents need to make sure that they are still focusing upon all children in their family. Showing all your children that you are interested in them and care for them is important. Children are much more likely to tell about abuse if they feel that they will be believed, cared for, not rejected and that the parent will do something to stop the behaviour. This applies to both a victim of abuse and also a young person who has abused.

What to watch for: possible signs that a child is being sexually abused

It is important to be aware of some of the possible signs children can display if they are experiencing sexual abuse. Such knowledge can help you pay attention to the needs of vulnerable children and to understand what to look for to help protect children in the future. It can also help you to think back to recognise and better understand any sexual abuse that the young person who has abused may have experienced in the past.

Any list of possible signs of sexual abuse should be seen as a guide only. Few of the signs that I suggest below are specific to sexual abuse and if your child displays them there may be innocent or non-abusive explanations. This is especially the case in the non-sexual behaviours and emotional signs I list below. If you notice any of the following signs you should not jump to conclusions one way or another, but keep an open mind and follow the advice given in the next section on what to do if you **do** suspect that a child is being abused. The greater the number of the following signs that appear to apply, the stronger your suspicion of sexual abuse should be.

Physical signs that may suggest a child is being sexually abused include:

- Presence of semen or semen stains in younger children's clothes or beds.
- Pregnancy in a child: especially young teenagers.
- Injury to a child's genital area or private parts.
- Bruising, soreness or redness of the genitals or bottom in boys and girls.

Signs in children's **sexual behaviour** that they may be experiencing sexual abuse include:

- A child who talks a lot about sexual acts. Resist the temptation of assuming that these are merely a product of the child's imagination.
- Sexually explicit drawings, e.g. a child drawing people having sexual intercourse, oral sex, or males with erect penis, especially if semen is drawn.
- A child whose play is very sexually oriented, e.g. a child at play showing dolls having sex or doing sexual things.
- A child who is sexually aggressive towards other children. Aggression is not normally found in normal childhood sexual experimentation.
- A child who talks in a sexually suggestive way, especially a young child to older children and adults.
- A child who shows sexual behaviours with animals.
- A child who cannot seem to stop masturbating, masturbates in inappropriate places or masturbates to the point of hurting herself.

- A child who puts objects into her vagina or anus.

Signs in children's **non-sexual behaviours** that they may be éxperiencing sexual abuse include:

- Problems with sleeping, nightmares and fear of going to bed, being distressed at the dark.
- Bed wetting and soiling, especially in children who have been dry and who start to wet again.
- A child who hurts herself. This includes suicide attempts or thoughts, e.g. a child who draws pictures of suicide or death, and self harm.
- Refusing to be left alone, especially with a particular person or people.
- Being frightened of a particular person, especially if this person has a history of abusing.
- A child who seems to develop a particular fear of men.
- A child who seems to be obsessed with fire or lighting fires (this is especially characteristic of boys who are being sexually abused).
- Any cruelty to animals (again this is especially common in boys who have been sexually abused).
- Eating disorders or problems (such as anorexia or bulimia).
- Running away from home.
- Any sudden or noticeable changes in behaviour.

Signs in **children's emotions** that they may be experiencing sexual abuse include their feeling:

- anxiety
- depression
- anger
- guilt

One of the difficulties in using these signs when thinking about a child who you know has been sexually abused in the past is whether these reflect the past abuse, or new and continuing abuse. You should be wary of new behaviours that emerge, and changes in your child's emotions.

Strategies to protect others in the community

Many of the ideas and pointers above relating to managing risk in families also apply to the wider community. For example, if it is important to restrict your child's play with younger children in the house, so it is important to consider how to restrict this in the community too.

It is clearly not possible to stop a young person who has abused having contact with all children, as children live in all communities. Simply walking down the street to the shop may put a young person in a position where he is passing children who may be younger, more vulnerable and potentially unaccompanied. Again, the degree to which these kinds of situations are risky for your child will vary according to how your child has abused in the past, where the abuse happened and who your child chose to abuse.

Very few young people need watching 24 hours a day in the community, and those that do should be being given specialist help and perhaps specialist accommodation. For most young people, taking sensible precautions to avoid high-risk situations and to manage other lower-risk situations is adequate. Your child should be asked to take some responsibility for agreeing to this and to avoid risk situations out of the house. For example, Stuart abused boys whilst playing with them in a local wood. Stuart's parents agreed with Stuart that he would not go to the wood again. This was possible as there was no reason for him to go there.

As a point of general principle, young people who have sexually abused should be prevented from walking past their victim's houses. Even if this is inconvenient, they should be required to take alternative routes to school or work. If the young person is out in the locality, you should always know where he is and who he is with. Having some kind of an agreement that your child reports to you regularly about what he has been doing is a good idea. This is clearly not what parents do in normal circumstances, but is necessary in that it gives your child a sense of having your support and gets him used to talking about risky situations.

Managing negative community responses

Unfortunately, many parents whose children have engaged in sexually problematic or abusive behaviours find that they meet a lot of negative feeling and responses from the communities in which they live. Many people have very strong feelings about sexual offenders and this is often fuelled by reports about 'paedophiles' in newspapers. Many people feel afraid that their own children are at risk and want to force the sexual offender away from their community. Few people understand the issues for children and young people who have sexually abused. For these reasons many families are forced to keep the abuse secret to avoid being targeted or feeling unsafe. Some families are required to move house into another area completely. Here are some ways of responding to such issues:

- If someone hears a rumour and asks you about it, you may wish to answer by stressing that there is a problem, adding that this is something you are working to resolve but making it clear that you cannot talk about the details. For example, you could say, 'that's not the whole truth, but there are some problems we are having at the moment that we are trying to sort out.'

- You should not feel forced to tell or be put on the spot. If you want to tell someone then be aware of the possible consequences and plan what you are going to say in advance.

- If you can tell a close friend or friends for support, then this may make the overall isolation easier to bear. Make sure that these people are trustworthy and know why it is important to keep the information safely.

- Don't feel guilty about keeping the details from people. Few families share all of their most difficult problems with people in the street.

- Remember that unnecessary secrecy is bad, but certain precautions to protect yourself, your children and your family are sensible.

- Talk to a social worker, police officer or other professional about this.

It is also important to agree what should be said and not said by others in your family. This particularly applies if a young person who was previously living with you is now living away from home for a while. What are you going to say when a neighbour asks you where your child is and why he is not living with you at the moment? Having an answer to questions like this is important. These are often called 'cover stories' by parents, for example:

> June's child, Karl, was in a children's home following his abuse of his sister. June was asked by her neighbours why her son wasn't in the family home

anymore. She was worried about the effect on her family if she told the real reason, so she said that Karl had moved because he had been violent towards her. When asked to give details about what exactly he had done, June said that she would rather not as it was painful for her, but reassured the neighbours that things were being done to help Karl. June was able to confide in her closest friend the real reasons for Karl's move.

June's cover story is a good example as it lets people know that something very serious had happened and was based in truth, as Karl had been physically violent towards her. It sensitively asked people not to ask more questions and all the family could use it. It also protected the sister who had been abused as she was not teased or asked hurtful questions by other children.

If you do need to think of a cover story it may be helpful to follow these guidelines:

- Don't say things that you will have to 'un-say' later on.
- Keep the cover story as simple as possible and as truthful as is safe.
- Avoid telling even more complicated stories as time passes.
- Stick to the story. Be consistent in what you say over time.
- Make sure that everyone in your family agrees to the cover story.

If you suspect or discover unknown or new abusive incidents

Very often this is the last thing that a parent wishes to hear or even to consider. However, as a parent who is offering support to your child, you are often in the frontline as far as new disclosures of abuse are concerned. You may see something which gives you strong reasons to believe that abuse is occurring or is about to occur. If this is the case, it is **vital** that you discuss this or report the information to a professional who will help to deal with this. Trying to cope with ongoing abuse alone by keeping it in your family is likely to lead to the abuse simply carrying on and can place an impossible burden on you as the parent. If you are not sure, but have suspicions from what you have seen in your child's behaviour, then talking to someone who has more experience than you have will help you to separate out the things you should and shouldn't be worried about. Talking to someone in these situations is not a sign of being a disloyal or distrustful parent. It is the sign of a responsible and caring parent.

If you find out about abuse that took place in the past but has stopped now (e.g. if your child tells you about another victim he abused):

- Don't assume that other people already know about this.
- Don't think that it's irrelevant because it's in the past. If this is about a new victim, then this victim may never have been offered any help to get over the abuse.
- Remember that this information might be another important part of the whole picture and may be crucial in helping your child's worker or therapist to better help your child to stop.

If you find out about new or current abuse:

- Don't panic or jump to conclusions. Keep calm.
- Don't think that telling will make it worse for your child.
- Remember the notion of the cycle of sexual assault. This shows how children can sometimes go back to their behaviours before breaking the cycle of abuse for good. Although there may be serious consequences for the victim and the young person too, all is not necessarily lost.
- Keep faith in the system to be able to deal with the new abuse and **report it**.

Summary points from this section

- Thinking about and doing something about risk situations is not a sign that you don't trust your child, but is responsive parenting. It shows you care about your child and other children.
- Thinking about how to deal effectively with risk in the family and community is the single most important thing you can do to support your child in a non-abusive lifestyle.
- Developing ways of dealing with situations according to how much risk they pose is an important way of finding balance in your life.
- The demands of monitoring are great. It is important to get some support. The young person should take some responsibility here too.
- Being alert to the signs of abuse, and being prepared to act on information you have, is a key way of reducing risk.

Questions to consider

- How good are the safety mechanisms and agreements you have in place at the moment both in relation to dealing with risky situations in your family and in the community?
- Can you distinguish between and justify the different levels of supervision and monitoring you have in place for different situations?
- How can the burden of monitoring be shared more fairly?

Exercise 19: Risk management planning in the home

Purpose. This exercise is designed to encourage you to plan with your child how risk will be managed in the home. It is designed to be filled in and agreed with the young person and to act as a kind of contract about how risks will be dealt with.

1. Situations of high risk to be **stopped or avoided**:

Describe the high risk situation	Why does it involve high risk?	How will the young person deal with or avoid this risk?	How will the strategy be monitored by the parent?
1.1 1.2 1.3 1.4 1.5			

2. Situations of lower risk to be **watched and monitored**:

Describe the lower risk situation	Why does it involve lower risk?	How will the young person deal with this situation?	How will the risk situation be monitored by the parent?
2.1 2.2 2.3 2.4 2.5			

3. Other things that you can agree to in the home in order to manage risk:

....

....

4. What the child should do if there is a problem or they are getting into difficulty:

....

....

5. How this agreement will be monitored by you as parents:

....

....

Exercise 20: Risk management planning outside the home

Purpose. This exercise encourages you to plan with your child how risk will be managed outside the home. It is designed to be filled in and agreed with the young person and to act as a kind of contract about how risks will be dealt with in the community.

1. Situations of high risk to be **stopped or avoided**:

Describe the high risk situation	Why does it involve high risk?	How will the young person deal with or avoid this risk?	How will the risk situation be monitored by the parent?
1.1			
1.2			
1.3			
1.4			
1.5			

2. Situations of lower risk to be **watched and monitored**:

Describe the lower risk situation	Why does it involve lower risk?	How will the young person deal with this situation?	How will the risk situation be monitored by the parent?
2.1			
2.2			
2.3			
2.4			
2.5			

3. Other things that you can agree to in order to manage risk outside the home or in the community:

....

....

4. What the child should do if there is a problem or they are getting into difficulty:

....

....

5. How this agreement will be monitored by you as parents:

....

....

Exercise 21: Dealing with risky or worrying situations: a monitoring sheet

Purpose. This exercise is designed to help you to record the ways in which you deal with worrying situations on a day-to-day basis. It may help you to think about how you responded, what was going through your head, what you did and how successful this was. In recording these things, you can build up an idea of things that work and help, so that you can use the most successful strategies in the future.

Use this sheet any time a risk or worrying situation occurs. Compare your ways of dealing with risk over time. Which ways appear to be more successful and why?

Date	What happened	What I was thinking	What I did	What was the effect of my actions	How successful were my actions

Chapter 6
Supporting the Child who has Sexually Abused

Working with Professionals
Helping professionals to help your child

This section is all about how you can work well with professionals. This can demand a lot of effort and patience both on your part and on the part of the professional. Your child's sexually abusive or inappropriate behaviour may have brought you and your family into close contact with professionals for the first time, or you may be used to having a social worker or psychologist involved in your family in the past. Whatever your previous experiences have been, working well with professionals involved with your child is one of the best ways you can help your child.

As we saw in Chapter 2, some parents have experienced difficulties in their relationships with professionals. There may be suspicions on both sides. Professionals can be uncertain about how much the young person was influenced by his family. Parents can be suspicious because of the way that professionals talk and the demands they make. Sometimes, parents can feel that their needs are being overlooked and that a 'professional steamroller' has come into the family.

You can help any workers involved in direct work with your child by:

- Providing as much detail as possible about your child's life history, even if you think this reflects badly on you. Being honest and realistic will give the professionals a much better sense of what your child has had to cope with in his life so far. (See the next section for questions to help you provide useful information to a professional working with your child).

- Supporting and encouraging your child to take part in any work being offered to them. This work will be difficult and demanding and your child may question why he has to do this or what the benefits of the work are. Parents can make all the difference to how co-operative a child is, how much effort he puts into the work and how much benefit he takes from the work. It is important not to be aggressive in your attempts to encourage your child to take part. Statements such as 'I will be so proud of you when you get through this work' and 'I know it must be very difficult for you, but this work will make all the difference and I am behind you all the way...' are firm and directive enough without being aggressive.

- Making sure that your child is living in a safe situation, including making sure that other children in your house and the community are as safe as possible.

- Being alert and keeping your eyes open for signs that your child may be falling back into abusive or problematic behaviours.

- Reporting any concerns you have and any information which could suggest that your child is returning to an abusive pathway.

- Keeping in touch with professionals and getting information from them.

It is important to remember that professionals, be they social workers, psychologists, psychiatrists or experts in sexual abuse work, cannot wave a magic wand to solve your child's problems. It is likely that you have much more direct contact with your child than any professional. The influence you have on your child is at least as great, if not greater than that of the professionals.

Providing helpful information for professionals

The following are questions that aid you in providing the kind of information that a professional might find helpful about your child, including his earlier life experiences and the development of any problems. The questions are drawn and developed from the work of Sutton (2000). Be as honest as possible when considering these questions, even though some may remind you of difficult or painful times from the past. Remember that these questions are meant to be a guide only. The professional may have other specific questions, or there may be other specific issues not covered here that you feel are important to share. Think the questions through carefully and write down anything that comes from answering them that may be useful for someone working with you and your family. This will give the professionals attempting to help your child a good foundation for the work:

a) Child's early life history:

- What were your circumstances when your child was conceived?
- Was your pregnancy normal and healthy? What were the difficulties, if any?
- Who did the child live with when born?
- Were there any medical difficulties for you or the child at birth?
- Did you experience any post-natal depression?
- Were there any medical difficulties for the child in his first year of life?

b) Child's general difficulties (non-sexual):

- What general problems does your child have?
- What age was the child when you first became aware of these problems?
- Did anything happen around that time that could be linked to the problem starting?
- Why do you think that your child has this problem?
- Have there been any family events that have had a serious impact on your child (e.g. someone leaving the family, serious illness, someone dying, etc.)?
- What has worried you most about your child as he has been growing up?
- How is your child's general behaviour?
- Which behaviours would you like to see more of?
- What good qualities does your child possess?
- How challenging has it been to be a parent for your child?
- How impulsive is your child?
- How does your child express anger?

c) Child's sexually abusive or problematic behaviour:

- What do you know of your child's sexual life history?
- What do you remember of your child's sexual behaviours as a small child?
- When was the first time you realised that there may be a problem with your child's sexual behaviour?

- How possible is it that your child has experienced sexual abuse? If possible, what do you suspect might have happened?
- What have you noticed about your child's sexually problematic behaviours? Do you have any clues to help with; when and where the behaviours take place, what your child is like beforehand, what triggers the behaviour, what your child is like afterwards?
- Why do you think that your child has behaved in this way?
- How serious do you think your child's sexual behaviours are and why?
- What do you think your child's level of sexual knowledge is and where has your child gained this knowledge?

d) Health and development:

- Do you have any concerns about your child's general health?
- Has your child had any mental health difficulties now or in the past?
- Has your child received any help from a psychologist or psychiatrist for any problems prior to the discovery of the sexually abusive behaviour?
- Has your child had any major illnesses or medical condition or spent any time in hospital?
- Does your child, as far as you know, drink alcohol or take any drugs? If yes, what do you know?
- What are your child's eating habits like now and in the past?
- What are your child's sleeping patterns? Do you have any concerns about this?
- When did your child enter puberty? How did you first realise this and what changes did you see?

e) Your child's self-esteem, confidence and identity:

- Before the sexual abuse took place, do you think that your child felt reasonably good about himself?
- What do you think your child thinks of himself now?
- Do you think that your child has any worries about his looks or body?
- Do you think your child has any worries about his sexuality?
- How confident is your child in new situations?

f) Family relationships:

- How does your child get on with other people in the family?
- What are the most important rules in your family?
- What enjoyable things do you do together as a family?
- What is the most common cause of family conflict?
- What has been the impact on the rest of your family of your child's sexually problematic or abusive behaviours?
- Who knows about the behaviours?

g) Relationships outside the family:

- How many close friends does your child have? Are the friends the same age and gender as your child?

- Does your child get on best with children younger than himself, young people the same age, or adults?
- If your child has few friends, do you think he is lonely?
- How much time does your child spend with friends in the house each week? (If there is a difference now and before the abuse was discovered, what is it?)
- How much time does your child spend with friends out of the house each week? (If there is a difference now and before the abuse was discovered, what is it?)
- When your child is out, how often do you know who your child is with, where he is and when he will be back?

What to ask and expect from professionals

It is in both your and your child's best interests if you can develop a good working relationship with professionals who are involved with your family. Professionals come in all shapes and sizes! However, parents generally have less power than the professionals who have the power of decision-making over the family. Going along with something just because a professional said it or putting up with treatment that is unfair, may not be the best thing in the longer-term.

Like all relationships, you will 'click' with some professionals better than others. However, there are certain things you should get and can expect from any professional who comes into your life as a result of sexual abuse. As a minimum, you should:

- Be given information about what is happening at all points.
- Have things explained clearly and be able to ask questions if you are unsure.
- Not feel pressured or pushed into agreeing to something that you are uncomfortable with.
- Be included and have a say in why certain decisions are being taken.
- Be treated respectfully as an adult.
- Be given an opportunity to give your views on your child and his behaviour.
- Be supported with the job of being a parent of a child who has a sexual behaviour problem.

If you feel that you are not being treated in these ways, you should be able to raise your concerns. It is generally best to do this in a non-aggressive way, so that the other person does not automatically feel threatened or defensive. For example, saying 'I'm sorry, but I don't feel that you are treating me with respect. I would like to say that...' or 'I am not sure that I understand that. Could you explain what you mean...' are perfectly reasonable ways of pointing out your concerns. If you feel that your child or you have been treated unfairly, you can make a complaint. Most professionals work in agencies which have written information for parents on how to complain. If you have not been given one of these at the beginning of the work, you could ring the organisation and ask to speak to someone who is senior to the person you are complaining about. Making a complaint should be the last resort though and you should have tried to talk things through with the person concerned beforehand.

Tips for working well with professionals

- Keep calm. If something is making you angry, let the person know exactly what it is, but say so calmly.
- Say what you are thinking.
- Ask questions if you are unsure. Seek out the information you need.
- Correct factual errors that you hear.

- Remember that the person concerned could be a useful source of help to you. Don't burn all your bridges at an early stage.
- Remember you have a vital role in any work with your child and your child's best interests will be better served by you working together with the professionals.
- If there are things you disagree with, say so and have your disagreement noted and acknowledged (e.g. in meetings).

Preparing for meetings with professionals

Feelings can run high in meetings. You may feel that you have little power or status amongst groups of trained professionals, but you should remember that you probably know your child better than anyone else and your contributions are therefore vital. It is helpful to prepare what you would like to ask and say in meetings with professionals before they take place. We can all go blank under pressure, so you should consider writing down some notes and any questions you have or points you wish to make. The following are suggestions about what you can do to get the most out of meetings with professionals:

- Read carefully any written information or reports which have been given to you beforehand.
- Look up or ask about any unfamiliar terms or technical language.
- Underline any points you would like to ask about, give your opinion about, or get more information on.
- Make a list of other things to say (see exercise on *Preparing for meetings with professionals* later in this section).

Summary points from this section

- Effective work with professionals can be a key way of gaining support for yourself and for your child.
- Parent and professional relationships can sometimes be tense as a result of the different perspectives and responsibilities felt by the people involved.
- Parents are a vital part of the professional system and should be able to contribute as fully as possible.
- Preparing for meetings and being clear about what it is you want to say can help deal with potentially overwhelming situations where you can feel powerless.

Questions to consider

- Do you always feel that you have been able to contribute as fully as possible to discussions with professionals about your child's situation?
- Are there ways in which you can prepare so that you can represent your position calmly and more effectively?

Exercise 22: Preparing for meetings with professionals

Purpose. This exercise is designed to help you prepare for meetings you may have with professionals, so that you can take part as fully as possible and offer your views and opinions.

Write down a list which covers the following points. Take the list with you to read from in the meeting.

1. I need to sort out or clarify the following things:

....

....

....

....

2. Things I disagree with ('I don't think it's correct to say...')

....

....

....

....

3. I want to give the following opinions:

....

....

....

....

4. Information I feel it might be helpful to offer:

....

....

....

....

5. Questions I want to ask (and who to ask):

....

....

....

....

The System and How to Contribute to it

There are two professional systems that you may come into contact with following your child's abuse. They are connected, in that a similar range of professionals work in both systems, although the law and policies governing each system is different and each has different aims and responsibilities. The major points are set down below, although each is significantly more complex than I can represent here and it is worth gaining the advice of professionals working with you about the implications of these systems for your own situation.

Key points about the Child Protection System

The *Child Protection System* in the UK is the name given to the arrangements made between all those professional agencies in a local area who are involved in working with children and who have a responsibility to collaborate to protect children from risk of harm or abuse. Each area has an Area Child Protection Committee (ACPC) which ensures that there is a local system in place to ensure agencies work together and co-operate in this way.

Examples of workers who form part of the Child Protection System are: social workers employed by the social services department or voluntary agencies (for example NSPCC), police officers, health visitors, medical doctors (either based in hospitals or GPs), Probation Officers. All of these people are required to share information and to co-operate to offer services aiming to **prevent** and **respond to** the abuse or harm of children.

Each local area has a set of written guidelines which all the above professionals need to follow. These guidelines stipulate what should happen if an allegation of child abuse comes to the attention of any of the agencies working in the area. Usually it is the responsibility of the police and the social services to look into such allegations and to investigate what course of action should be taken. ACPCs have arrangements to hold meetings, called case conferences, between the professionals where allegations of harm or abuse to children are investigated. It may be that your child's sexually abusive behaviour has led to an investigation and a case conference under the local ACPC arrangements. You should be invited to attend the case conference, put forward your views, and listen to the views of other people. You may be asked to leave the room when decisions are made. A child who is the subject of a case conference is invited where appropriate.

Case conferences have only limited powers to make decisions and recommendations. They can decide to place a child's name on the local 'Child Protection Register'. This is a list of children who have been assessed as at risk of harm or abuse and who need professional support, help or protection. A child on the child protection register is allocated a social worker who co-ordinates services to reduce the risk of harm to the child. Review meetings are held every six months until the core group of professionals working with the child and family agrees that the risks have been reduced.

Key points about the criminal justice system

Your child's sexually abusive behaviour may also have brought you into contact with the criminal justice and court system. In law, no child under the age of ten can be found guilty of a criminal offence. At age eighteen a young person is treated as an adult by the law and comes under the same court system as all adults. Between ten and seventeen, young people are dealt with by the Youth Court. The legal system is very complicated and it is not possible here to provide detailed information either about how it works or the range of possible consequences for your child. Below are some of the key points of which parents should be aware. If your child's behaviour brings him to the attention of the courts, it is vital to get legal advice.

Central to the criminal justice system, as it affects young people who have committed criminal offences, is the position of local Youth Offending Teams (YOTs). These teams are made up of social workers, police officers, psychologists, etc., all of whom are specifically experienced in work with young people who have committed offences. If your child needs to go to court, a member of the YOT team will write a report for the court which lays down the circumstances surrounding the offence and makes a recommendation to the court.

If your child is convicted of an offence, the court will consider factors such as the age of the child and the court's views about the seriousness of the offence before deciding from a range of options. Courts can order:

- The payment of a fine or money for compensation (where the parent or guardian has to pay).
- A Reparation or Action Plan Order (where the child has to carry out activities or follow the court's instructions for a period of time under the supervision of a professional).
- A Parenting Order (see below).
- For a young person who has sexually offended the making of a Supervision Order, which can be up to a maximum of three years, is more common. Here the court can attach a wide range of requirements to the order, for example to direct the young person to attend for treatment. Supervision is by a social worker, probation officer or a member of a youth offending team.
- Probation Orders can be made for young people aged 16 and 17. The court may select any period from six months to three years. The young person is placed under the supervision of a probation officer. There are a range of conditions that a court can attach to the order, including saying where a young person should live and what treatment he should have.

The Youth Court is now able to consider placing parents of young people who appear in the Youth Court on a Parenting Order. A Parenting Order requires parents to attend guidance and support sessions to receive help in dealing with their children. The aim of a Parenting Order is to help and support parents when their children get into trouble. A Parenting Order can have two parts to it:

1. It can require you to go to counselling or guidance sessions to receive help in dealing with your child. This will involve weekly sessions for no longer than three months.
2. A court may also require you to control your child's behaviour for up to twelve months. In such cases, the court appoints a responsible officer (a social worker, a probation officer or a member of the Youth Offending Team), whose responsibility it is to supervise the requirements of the order. Not to go ahead with these requirements is a criminal offence and you could be fined up to £1000 as a result.

How the sex offender register works and the implications for parents

Since the Sex Offenders Act 1997 came into force anyone who has been convicted of or cautioned for sexual offences must register with the police in their area and must keep the police informed about their whereabouts. The police use the information on the sex offender register to assess the risk that individuals might be presenting and to monitor those who the police feel present a large risk.

Anyone convicted of an offence that requires registration is given a certificate by the Court which says what they must do to register. If this happens to your child, you must make sure you inform the local police of your child's name, date of birth and address within 14 days of conviction. Any changes of address after that must be given to the police within 14 days of the change. If your child is going to stay at a different address for 14 days or longer in any twelve-month period this information must also be given to the police. The easiest way to give this information is to go into the police station nearest to where your child is living, although you can also let the police know in writing.

The length of time for which your child is placed on the sex offender register depends upon the length of the sentence given out. For young people under the age of 18 years, the length of time they have to register is half of what it would be for an adult who had been convicted of a similar offence, as follows:

Length of sentence	Length of requirement for a young person to register on the Sex Offender Register
Hospital (restriction order) More than 30 months custody Six months to 30 months custody Less than six months custody Non custodial sentence or caution	Forever Forever Five years Three and a half years Two and a half years

For every young person on the register the police undertake a risk assessment to weigh up the level of risk that the young person may pose in the community and more specifically the immediate risk to anyone with whom the young person may be having contact. The police are likely to carry out a home visit to do this and to make sure that the information they have been provided with is accurate. They will then share the information they gather with other professionals who may then draw up a plan for managing risks.

If the police are concerned that someone who already has a conviction or caution for a sexual offence is behaving in such a way in the community that the public needs protecting from this person, they can apply for a Sex Offender Order, which will prevent the person from doing the things or going to the places associated with the risk. Where young people aged ten to eighteen are concerned, Sex Offender Orders should only be made in exceptional circumstances and the police would have to liaise with the local Youth Offending Team and Social Services Department.

What a criminal conviction for a sex offence means for your child's future legal status

There are long-term implications for your child of having a conviction or a caution (either a warning or reprimand) for a sexual offence. Your child will not be able to go into certain professions and is likely to have to declare his conviction when applying for a range of jobs. It will mean that your child will not be able to follow certain careers, most notably those that involve working with children or vulnerable adults, e.g. teaching. Unlike other offences which are 'spent' after a period of time, sexual offences need to be disclosed forever. Realising this often causes distress to young people and parents. Your child may need to reassess his ambitions and career plans as a result. If the young person subsequently has a relationship with someone who has a child, or has children of his own, he may come to the attention of the authorities again and another risk assessment may be carried out. All of this might seem very difficult and hopeless, but adults can, nevertheless, lead meaningful and responsible lives without being haunted by an offence that happened in the past.

What 'Treatment' Work Entails

As discussed in the first chapter, there are many terms which may be used in order to describe the kind of work which is offered to your child as a result of his sexually abusive behaviour. Additionally, a range of people as diverse as a social worker, Youth Offending Team member, psychologist or psychiatrist may offer this work. Irrespective of the professional label each person holds, this person should be experienced and knowledgeable in working with young people who have sexually abused and should be able to explain to you how they work. Some questions you might like to ask are:

- How is the person qualified and experienced to do this work?
- How does the person work and what theories and methods does she use?
- Who will be involved?
- How often will your child be seen?
- What information will you be given about what happens in the work? Who else will be told? Will you get copies of written reports?
- How will the young person's progress in the work be assessed and the work reviewed?
- What can you and others do outside of the sessions to help with the work?
- What role can you play in the work?
- Will there be any family sessions?
- How can you support the young person in the work?
- Will you get advice on managing risk?
- What does the worker expect to be different at the end of the work?
- What if there is a disagreement or you wish to make a complaint?

Getting answers to these questions will help you to understand the work being suggested and to contribute as fully as you can.

How long will 'treatment' take?

It is worth remembering that there are no 'quick fixes' in work on sexually abusive behaviour. As we have seen earlier in the book, the development of such behaviours in young people is often complex and long-term and, as a result, 'treatment' work can also be longer term. Anywhere between six and eighteen months is a common amount of time. It is also important to realise that a professional carrying out even a long-term piece of work with your child can only go so far. Parents are often the key to whether any programme of work is successful or not. If the messages from the work are reinforced through the actions of parents and others at home, then this supports the work. For example, if one of the themes of the treatment work is the need for the young person to take risk situations seriously, and the young person sees that this is reflected in how seriously his parents are taking this issue in the family, this will help to reinforce the work. However, if the risk is not taken seriously at home, this is likely to undermine or dilute the effectiveness of the work. As this example shows, professionals and parents working together and being in tune with each other is the best option.

How can I help?

Even though your direct involvement in the work may be limited, it may be useful to think of yourself as part of a 'helping team' for your child. This is an approach which has been developed successfully at the Kaleidoscope project in Sunderland. As part of this team, you will need information and regular updates about progress in the work, so that you can be aware of your child's ongoing needs when he is with you. However, you should also pass on any important news and information that you have to the workers. All members of the young person's helping team need to agree what information is going to be shared, how it will be shared and how regularly. It is also important to recognise that working on sexually abusive behaviour is likely to be difficult and painful for your child. Most young people do not wish to talk in detail to their parents following sessions about their content, but appreciate it when a parent demonstrates support and concern by enquiring about their feelings.

What sort of treatment is it?

Treatment work might be offered in a number of ways. It may be that your child is offered a place in a therapeutic group which is made up of other young people who have sexually abused, or they may be offered work on his own. Parents sometimes have concerns that a groupwork programme will simply encourage their child to mix with other young people and learn new ways of abusing from them. However, groupwork has been seen as a particularly effective way of working with young people who sexually abuse as it gives them an opportunity to see other young people who are at different stages in the work and to learn from their example. Additionally, for a young person who is stuck with abusive or distorted attitudes, the example of other young people who have successfully been able to challenge such attitudes can be helpful. More than anything, being in a group can give a young person a sense that he is not alone in having done something so serious and harmful. Both the support and the challenge that can be given by peers can be very much more powerful than that of an adult. However, groupwork must be properly structured and delivered by professionals.

If two people are working with your child, it is often the case that this will be a man and a woman together as this is seen as a good way of teaching a young person about how men and women can work together positively and can help the young person to challenge any sexist or distorted thoughts he may have about gender, particularly young men who may have hostile thoughts about women. Whether your child is offered individual or groupwork, it is helpful for you to have an understanding about the theories being used, the aims of the work and how it is designed to encourage your child to change his sexually abusive behaviour. Different methods are used by projects across the country, but are most likely to be described as 'cognitive behavioural' in their focus.

The ideas behind 'cognitive behavioural' approach

Cognitive behavioural approaches to work with young people who sexually abuse combine an emphasis on influencing a person's patterns of thought (known traditionally as 'cognitive therapy') with an emphasis on changing a person's behaviour (known as 'behavioural therapy'). A central idea of a cognitive behavioural approach is that a young person's thoughts, emotions, behaviours and sexual responses are inter-connected. Changing one of these elements will influence the others. Key ideas are:

- Thoughts can lead to emotions and behaviour.
- Sexually abusive behaviour is fuelled by distorted or problematic thinking and emotional difficulties.
- The likelihood of sexually abusive behaviour can be reduced by changing problem thoughts and by learning to deal with difficult feelings.

Cognitive behavioural approaches therefore aim to give young people who have sexually abused the tools that are necessary to deal with risk situations and to move away from problematic patterns of thinking or abusive patterns of behaviour. Parts of a cognitive behavioural approach to young people who abuse typically include:

- Teaching young people about sexual aggression, why people commit sexual abuse and who are the victims of abuse.

- Teaching young people about healthy sexuality and how to express their sexuality safely and appropriately. This might be by considering the qualities of a good relationship, thinking about how to find an appropriate partner, thinking about non-abusive sexual situations and how to deal with them.

- Encouraging young people to develop healthy attitudes and to express their feelings. This depends on the particular feelings that accompanied young people's abusive behaviour, but if they have problems with expressing anger, the work should help them cope with difficult situations without taking out anger on other people.

- Looking in very close detail at the connected thoughts, feelings and behaviours involved in a young person's sexually abusive behaviour. This means working with young people to help them identify and understand their own pathways into abusive behaviour and their patterns of abuse. Many projects doing this work use the idea of the cycle of sexually abusive behaviour, as described in Chapter 3.

- Looking back at the child's own past and thinking about influences on his thoughts, feelings and behaviours. This could involve looking at abuse that the young person has experienced himself and the feelings and beliefs that this left with the young person.

- Understanding and changing distorted thoughts to more healthy and positive thoughts. For example, understanding that young children cannot consent to having sex with teenagers. The negative thoughts that need changing may not be sexual in nature, for example, young people who believe that it is fine for males to be physically aggressive or violent.

- Victim awareness and apology work. This area of work involves the young person in understanding why it is that they have hurt his victim. Typically, this is done by asking the young person to see the abuse from the victim's perspective, sometimes writing letters to their victims, though these letters are written just for the work and are not sent, as this would be harmful and inappropriate for the victim.

- Changing deviant arousal patterns. Some young people who have abused have developed problematic patterns of sexual arousal (e.g. to children), which last even though the young person realises that the abusive behaviour is wrong. Some workers in this field use some specialised techniques to help change the young person's patterns of arousal. For example, such techniques might involve teaching the young person to introduce negative endings to any sexual fantasies they have about abusive sex.

- Problem solving and developing the young person's ability to deal with situations of stress and difficulty. This is not restricted to sexual situations. In trying to help your child to better cope with everyday problems and stresses in their life, the work aims to make it less likely that he will fall back into sexually abusive behaviour as a way of trying to make himself feel better. In particular, the work might try to help your child become assertive and to manage anger positively.

- Improving your child's social skills and self-esteem. As we have seen, many young people who have abused have a very low opinion of themselves. This can be a result of the combined experiences of the young person before the abuse took place or, indeed, because the whole process of the abuse coming to the attention of others has knocked the young person's confidence even further. This aspect of the work is therefore about helping a young person relate better to others. There is a limit to the extent that this can be achieved in the confines of the therapy room. Often, workers rely on you as parents to help with this area by encouraging the young person to take responsibility appropriately in other areas of life and to become involved in appropriate activities.

- **Relapse prevention skills.** This technical term refers to the skills a young person needs to help him stay away from sexually abusive behaviour. This involves working with your child to raise your child's awareness of risk situations and being very clear about what to do in such situations to avoid slipping back into abusive behaviour or responding in a way which could lead to abuse.

Summary points from this section

- 'Treatment' work is a good way of helping a young person to face up to the abuse and to reduce the risk that he will abuse again.

- On its own and without attention to other bits of a young person's life, the impact of such work will be limited.

- There needs to be consistency between the work and the messages given at home.

Questions to consider

- How much do you know of what is being done with your child, if he is being offered treatment work?

- What else do you need to know in order to make sure that you are reinforcing the messages in the work?

- What information can you give to those offering any work about how your child is at home on a day-to-day basis, to help them make their work relevant?

Your Contribution as a Parent to 'Treatment' Work

You may feel that treatment work is so specialist that there is little you can do in order to contribute. However, you have a vital role in all aspects of the work, and, as outlined above, cognitive behavioural work needs to be backed up by practical day-to-day help and support, as the young person deals with situations in his life. It may be helpful to distinguish between the things you can do to support your child's individual work and the direct contribution you may have in work offered to you as a wider family group.

Contributing to your child's individual work

You can help your child by ensuring that he attends for sessions on time and by ensuring that the work is given high priority. It is important to give your child positive messages about how pleased you are that he is going ahead with the work. If your child says things which denigrate or 'rubbish' the work or the workers offering it, it is helpful not to agree with this, but to stress that you think that the work is vital and that you want the young person to take it seriously. The work can provoke strong feelings in young people and sometimes they take out these feelings on the workers, who may be encouraging young people to face things that they would rather continue to avoid.

You can also support the work by being available to talk to your child about any issues raised in sessions. You should make some statements which lay the foundation for your child to feel able to approach you. Even if your child does not do this, you will have communicated your support to your child. Often, if you do not offer this, your child will simply think that you are not willing to talk. You could say something like 'I am not going to keep asking you, but if you would like to talk any time about the abuse or the work you are doing, I'll be here to listen.' As the work progresses, it may be important to take a more direct role, especially if your child is going to be returned home after having lived away for some time.

Contributing to family sessions

If your child is being offered a service to work on his sexually abusive behaviour, it is now commonplace for an offer of family work to be made, in addition to individual work with your child. In most cases, family sessions refer to the young person and parents working together in some form to help make the situation safe (especially if the child is living at home) and to meet the child's needs. At the Kaleidoscope project, for example, family sessions are offered throughout the time that a child is offered individual work. Sometimes, these are sessions with parents alone, and sometimes, parents and the young person jointly. Some parents feel understandably anxious and uncertain about becoming involved in such work. However, such sessions can be very helpful to you as well as your child. Young people can often be supported in talking to their parents about their feelings in family sessions in a way which is not possible in the course of normal family life.

Sometimes, particularly when the work is in its final stages, other family members may be invited to join family work sessions. Such decisions need careful thought and, in particular, brothers and sisters of the young person who has abused should not be pressured to take part in any family work, irrespective of whether they are victims. Commonly, family sessions provide an opportunity to:

- Talk to your child in a supported setting about the work he has been doing.
- Add your views to help or inform the work being offered individually to your child.

- Give your child an opportunity to say things that are difficult at home and to let you know what he feels the progress has been.
- Talk about family problems or issues that need to be sorted out.
- Give everyone an opportunity to safely express feelings in a supported way.

When family sessions go well, they can sometimes prove to be the most important turning point for families in facing up to the abuse and in looking to the future:

> Sandra and her son Darren, aged 14, were offered some joint sessions together after Darren had worked individually on his abusive behaviour for almost a year. It had been assumed by Darren's worker that joint sessions were not so necessary as Darren had continued to have a good deal of contact with Sandra after the abuse and they had a good relationship. However, family sessions which were initially seen as important only in terms of planning Darren's move back home, proved to be a turning point. With the support of the worker concerned, both Sandra and Darren were able to talk about their feelings in a way which neither had felt possible before. The sessions were safe and both Sandra and Darren were able to ask about difficult aspects of the abuse and the past without having to 'take these home'. Darren told his mother about the work he had done on identifying his pattern of abusive behaviour. Sandra said that it was only when she heard this that she was able to make sense of the last year.

This example shows the potential benefit of structured and supported family work. If you have a professional involved in working with your child on his sexually abusive behaviour and you are not offered such a service, you can ask about the possibility of building such sessions into the work.

Supporting your Child in Finding a Healthy Sexuality

After the abuse, it is very likely that your child will be confused about sex and sexual matters. You should not assume that, because your child has been involved in sexual acts before, that they have all the answers about sex, or that they have a good sense of what sex involves. Any work conducted with your child which has helped to control his sexually abusive behaviour will not have taken away the young person's sexuality. Your child will still have sexual thoughts, feelings and urges.

Indeed, now that the abuse has come out into the open, it may be less likely that your child will be able to ask about sexual problems or worries, as he might not wish to open up the pain of the abuse again. This is particularly true if your child knows that the abuse has hurt you. Your child might think that raising the subject of sex might be seen to be a sign that he is still at risk of abusing. If your child does talk to you or show evidence that he has ongoing sexual thoughts or feelings, you shouldn't assume that these are inappropriate. These sexual thoughts or worries might be about perfectly normal and healthy sexual matters, a part of your child creating a healthy and non-abusive future. This is demonstrated in this case example:

> Safina was the mother of a 17-year-old young man who had sexually abused a younger girl in the community but who had successfully completed a two-year period of work on his abusive behaviours. When she changed her child's bedclothes, Safina was distraught about seeing evidence of her child masturbating. She wondered if this meant that the work had been unsuccessful and if it was a sign that he was going to abuse again.

The subject of sex causes embarrassment in many parent-child relationships, even when there has been no history of sexual abuse. For parents of children who have abused sexually, any reference to sex, or their child's ongoing sexual thoughts, can be very worrying and can reawaken painful memories of the abuse, as it did for Safina.

Talking about sex

The process of sexually abusing someone else can knock off course a young person's sexual development. However, staying clear of sex and sexual relationships is not a realistic long-term choice for your child. Sooner or later, he will start to have sexual relationships. It might be wise for young people who have abused to avoid rushing into sexual intercourse with a girlfriend or boyfriend. However, sexual expression and healthy sexuality does not stop with full sex, and involves fantasising, masturbating, touching and oral sex. Whatever the context of his abusive behaviour, and however distant is the possibility of your child entering into a non-abusive sexual relationship, he needs to have information about responsible and safe sexual expression. This includes knowing about pregnancy, and contraception, how to use condoms, and the facts about HIV/AIDS and other sexually transmitted diseases. If you do not have information about these things, you can get it through a library or health centre or family planning clinic.

It may be difficult for you to talk to your child about sex now that you know he has abused, especially if you were not used to doing this before the abuse was discovered. You may feel that talking about sex makes it more likely that the abuse will happen again, but as I noted earlier in the book, studies show this not to be the case. Talking about sex in a mature way and stressing responsible sexual behaviour does not increase sexual activity, nor does it make it more likely that your child will re-offend sexually.

At the same time, you should not feel forced to be the main support for your child on sexual matters. If this is too painful, it may be wise to limit your role and to ensure that your child has other opportunities to get this help. If you do feel that this is something you can offer, you can prepare yourself to support your child's healthy sexual expression as follows:

- Acknowledge to your child that he will continue to have sexual urges, thoughts and feelings and that you understand these to be natural and OK, so long as they are not abusive.
- Talk with your child about girlfriend or boyfriend relationships.
- Don't turn off TV programmes with a normal level of sexual content (i.e. non-pornographic, non-adult). Use this, occasionally, as an opportunity to check how your child is coping with sex and sexuality in his day-to-day life.
- Give your child permission to ask questions about sexual things that he does not understand. Make it clear that you see this as an important way your child can face the future without abuse, rather than a sign of risk.
- Answer questions about sex honestly and accurately. If you do not know something, say so and agree to find out (preferably together).
- Stress to your child that he can say no to sex and that this does not make him different to other young people.
- Do not just focus on the mechanics of sex, but include the emotional side and pleasures of sex.

If all this is difficult, remember:

- To take things slowly. Don't rush into saying everything at once.
- To create an open climate, where your child sees that you are relaxed and can come back and talk to you again.
- To seek support for yourself, especially if this subject matter raises issues about your own sexual history and experiences.
- If you feel you have not responded well, or have got something wrong, go back to your child and correct yourself.

Although it may not feel like it now, your child's sexuality and relationships need not always be a matter of concern or worry, and supporting your child can be a way of growing closer following abuse.

What is sexual orientation?

Sexual orientation is a term which describes a person's emotional and sexual attraction to another person. **Heterosexual** people can experience sexual and emotional attraction to people of the opposite sex. People with a heterosexual orientation (both men and women) are sometimes referred to as 'straight'. **Homosexual** people can experience sexual and emotional attraction to people of the same sex. People who have a homosexual orientation are sometimes referred to as 'gay' (both men and women) or as 'lesbian' (women only). **Bisexual** people can experience sexual and emotional attraction to both their own sex and the opposite sex. Sexual orientation is different from sexual behaviour because it refers to feelings and identity: how people see themselves. People may or may not express their sexual orientation in their behaviours. Equally, people's sexual behaviour may not represent their sexuality. So, if your child has sexually abused a child of the same sex, this does not necessarily mean that he is gay. Similarly, a young person who abuses a child of the opposite sex should not be assumed to be straight. Separating non-abusive sexual orientation from the abuse of sexuality is an important task for your child in finding a healthy and sexually fulfilling future.

Whilst a person's sexual orientation can be influenced by experiences, most researchers today agree that sexual orientation is not something that we chose, but it is set biologically. In other words, it is inborn. Homosexuality, heterosexuality and bisexuality are all acceptable forms of sexual orientation, as long as they are expressed in a non-abusive way. No single orientation is better than another, as long as the person is comfortable with his or her orientation. Young people who have abused need to see that their parents value them as individuals regardless of, and because of, the nature of their healthy sexual orientation. Because of the stigma and prejudice generally held against gay people, young people who have abused may feel confused or ashamed if they are gay and worry that 'coming out' will make people think they are going to continue to abuse.

Summary points from this section

- Young people's sexual needs do not disappear just because they have been caught abusing.
- Finding a positive and healthy sense of sexuality, including a safe way of meeting their sexual needs, is a key task for all young people who sexually abuse.
- Sex and sexuality are often shameful and embarrassing subjects for all young people, especially if a young person has sexually abused.
- It is important for parents to distinguish the abuse of sexuality from their child's healthy sexual orientation, regardless of whether this is as straight, gay or bisexual.

Questions to consider:

- What are all the positive things you could do to help your child feel good about his sexual orientation?
- What information might you need to do this?

Exercise 23: Identifying the contribution you can make to your child's work

Purpose. This exercise is designed to help you to look more closely at the things you can do to help your child in any work being undertaken with him.

1. Things I can do to support the work are:

....

....

....

....

2. Ways in which I can help my child:

....

....

....

....

3. Ways in which I can play a part:

....

....

....

....

4. Family sessions could involve:

....

....

....

....

5. We could use family sessions to talk about the following:

....

....

....

....

Exercise 24: Preparing to talk to your child about sex

Purpose. This exercise provides you with an opportunity to consider how you can support your child by talking about sexual things.

1. Talking to your child about sex and healthy sexual expression is easier if you are prepared. Use the space below to write down the six key messages about healthy sexuality that you would like to communicate to your child at this point in time (the examples below may help). This should give you a sense of what the most important issues are for you currently.

Examples:
- Your beliefs about sex.
- What you hope for your child sexually now and in the future.
- What's OK for adolescents to engage in.
- Safer sex and sexual health.
- Sex and relationships.
- Masturbation.

1.1

....

....

1.2

....

....

1.3

....

....

1.4

....

....

1.5

....

....

1.6

....

....

2. Imagine yourself discussing each topic you have listed (one at a time) with your child. Think about where, when and what you would say and how you would say it. Think about what your child would say in response. Imagine how you both would look.

3. Look back at your list and put two ticks against any of the items that you would feel totally comfortable about discussing, one against those that you would feel a bit comfortable about and none against any which you wouldn't be comfortable with. What would help you with those items that you are less comfortable about?

4. If you have a partner who shares the parenting task with you, complete this exercise alone and then compare the things you have come up with. How similar are your messages and your 'comfortable' levels? What does this say about the parenting roles each of you takes on? How consistent are you in the messages you give your child?

Exercise 25: Hopes for your child's sexual future

Purpose. This exercise is designed to help you think through the hopes you have for your child, his sexuality now, and in the future, and what you can do to offer support and help to give your child the best opportunity to reach his own goals.

Finding out about your child's sexually abusive behaviour can affect your hopes about your child's future in all kinds of ways. Thinking about your child having sexual relationships may be the last thing you want to do now. However, it is important to have some ideas about how you would like your child's healthy sexual behaviour and relationships to be in the future, as you have a crucial role in helping your child to develop a sense of healthy sexual self.

1. Write down the five most important hopes you have for your child's sexual future:

1.1

1.2

1.3

1.4

1.5

2. Think about the things you have written and consider the following questions:
• How realistic are the hopes that you have set?
• Is your child aware of your hopes? Would he be surprised if you voiced your hopes? Which of the hopes would it be helpful for your child to know about now and which would not be helpful?
• Do you imagine that your child shares your hopes?
• What practical and emotional support could you offer to help your child to reach these goals? What else does your child need?

Chapter 7
The Future

Facing the Future with Hope

This book has tried to emphasise that you can have a future following your child's sexually abusive behaviour. This includes you as a parent, your family and your child. However painful the abuse has been, with the right kind of intervention, support, monitoring and care you can move beyond the crisis to find 'balance' in your life. I use the notion of balance carefully. It is not going to be possible, nor should you try, to forget about the abuse or to convince yourself, or your child, that it has never happened. The abuse will always be a part of your story as a parent, and of your child's history.

At the same time, it is important to be able to see the future with some optimism. Some of the families I have worked with, and whose stories I have used, are living examples of this. At the beginning of their journeys, their sense of desolation and confusion meant that they could not see beyond the horror of the abuse. Towards the end of our work together though, some of these parents and families had been able to turn the corner and not only get back to the way of life they had before the abuse, but to go beyond this into new positive ways of living as a family. For example:

- Susan and Mark, whose teenage son abused their younger son, found that their life and relationship with each other and their children had improved as a consequence of having to look so closely into some of the negative aspects of their family.

- Madge, whose son abused children in the community, was able to free herself from her 15-year-long abusive marriage and said she only found out who she really was as a result.

There are, of course, other examples of families who have not been able to find this degree of 'balance' in their lives following the abuse. However, I hope that you can find ways of making the best of your own situation. You cannot expect to feel optimistic about the future in the early stages of this journey; but you should try to hold onto the hope that you and your family can survive the experience intact and stronger than before.

The second important consideration here is your child. Again, I have tried to communicate a difficult balance in this book, between the need to take your child's sexually abusive behaviour very seriously and at the same time to understand, accept, support and value your child, as a child. I have stressed that it is important not to let the lessons you have learnt slip away and to allow your child to drift back into destructive, problematic or abusive patterns of behaviour.

'Once an abuser always an abuser?' This is the kind of statement sometimes made about young people who have abused. This book has tried to emphasise that this statement need not apply. In identifying risk issues and retaining a level of awareness about risk and responsible behaviour, whilst at the same time not allowing the abuse to dominate life for you and your family, you can give your child the best opportunity to have an abuse-free future.

When is it right to consider reuniting your family?

If your child has moved away from home after the abuse, there will come a time when you may need to consider whether the circumstances are right for the child to return to live with you. This is not a straightforward question and will depend on a number of factors, including:

- How much progress your child has shown in any work offered.
- The degree of ongoing risk your child presents.
- Your family's circumstances (e.g. the accommodation you have).
- How the abuse was committed in the first place (e.g. whether the victim was a family member).
- How vulnerable any other children in the family are.
- The strength of any supervision plans in place.

The decision as to *whether* and *when* to rehabilitate a young person who has abused a sibling is particularly difficult. When abused siblings are asked whether they want their brother or sister to return, they almost always say 'yes'. Sometimes parents attach a great deal of importance to this without recognising it is almost impossible for them to answer 'no' to this question. Most siblings who have been abused **do** want their brother or sister to return, but crucially, they want them not to hurt them again. They need reassurance that they are safe. They need to see practical evidence of change and to hear that they will be believed if they were to speak out about abuse in the future. In the face of the huge pressure that so often is placed on siblings to conform to plans to bring the young person back into the home or to say 'yes' to such plans, there are a range of considerations that should inform decisions about rehabilitation.

The following are the *best conditions* that would enable a child, who has left the family home because of his sexual abuse, to return home (adapted from Hackett, Print and Dey, 1998).

The young person who has sexually abused has been able to:

- Take full responsibility for the sexual abuse.
- Understand the impact of his behaviour on the victim and has been able to express concern for the victim.
- Is sorry for the abuse and, where appropriate, has apologised.
- Understand why they sexually abused.
- Realise what ongoing risk situations are and can talk about these to you as parents and get help outside the family if necessary.

You as parents have been able to:

- Put the victim's needs for protection first.
- Talk to your child and express your feelings about the abuse.
- Discuss the impact of the abuse upon yourselves with your partner.
- See your child as responsible and do not blame the victim.
- Accept the differing needs of the victim, and the young person who has abused, and yet feel that there is a place for meeting both in your family.
- Make any necessary changes in your parenting style and skills, and your family.
- See the importance of continuing to monitor risk situations.

The victim (if the victim is a sibling):

- Has been able to acknowledge and discuss the sexual abuse.
- Knows that the abuse was not her fault and does not blame herself for the young person getting into trouble.
- Wants the young person who has abused to be re-united with the whole family.
- Is confident that she could report any further abuse and knows who she could talk to.
- Feels safe and protected in the home even if the brother or sister who abused is there.

The whole family agrees that:

- The young person should come home.
- Everyone needing or wanting help has had it offered. All the work needed has been done or is sufficiently underway to allow confidence that it will be successfully completed.
- Possible risk situations have been shared and there is a protection plan in place, which everybody agrees to stick to and which involves the support of professionals or others outside of the family.
- Boundaries are strong in the family and people are open with each other.
- Any relationship difficulties have been talked about and progress made.
- Any physical issues in the home requiring attention have been addressed, e.g. location of bedrooms, sleeping arrangements, etc.

If your child comes home, it is best to do this in a planned way, rather than as an emergency or, in other words, not just because something has happened to end his placement and there are no other options. A written plan should be drawn up which states clearly what is expected of the young person, situations to be avoided, and how risk is to be managed in the family. It is best to consider a slow introduction back home. Trial runs are a good way of making changes, where those who are affected (other siblings, victims and the young person who has abused etc.) are consulted about their views on how changes are progressing.

About the end of professional intervention

You face different challenges at the end of your journey than at the beginning. In particular, the formal end of professional involvement in the life of your child marks an important stage. If the work has been completed and is being ended in a planned way, this should signal that all has been done to try to help your child. It is now down to your child to take full responsibility for his behaviour and to use the knowledge and skills he has gained throughout the work to good effect.

It can be useful to think back and weigh up what has changed since the time that the abuse was discovered. What has improved and what is still difficult? If there is positive change, it is helpful to recognise this for yourself and to give your child credit and praise for what he has achieved. In most circumstances, there will still be some problems or worries, but these will be manageable. It is also important to carry on considering your child as a whole person. For example, studies show that young people who sexually abuse others are more likely to get into trouble with the police in the future for non-sexual crimes than sexual ones (Worling and Curwen, 2000). You should be focused on all aspects of your child's development and behaviour, not just the sexual part.

If you have ever tried to give up any 'addictive' pattern of behaviour, for example smoking or drinking, then you will know that maintaining or keeping up the change needs different skills and tactics than giving up the behaviour in the first place. This is the same with your child's sexually abusive behaviour. Young people and, indeed, families can come to depend upon the support of professionals to help with all kinds of problems and emotional difficulties in the aftermath of sexual abuse. Whilst the end of professional input into the life of your child or your family is an important step in facing the future, it may also lead to fear and anxiety. Such fears can include 'will we cope alone and without support?' and 'will my child fall back into problem or abusive behaviours?'

And afterwards...

Most professionals who offer a service for young people who sexually abuse will offer some kind of follow-up to the work which they have completed. Sometimes the work may have been such a struggle that families and young people simply wish to move on and break contact with professionals. However, taking up the option of any follow-up work or contact with a professional who has been involved is a good idea. This may include an informal meeting where you talk about progress, what your child has been doing and whether the conditions or risk management plans that were put in place at the end of the work are being maintained. Such meetings can also provide an opportunity to talk about any issues that have been concerning you or your child. Most projects that have worked with a young person over a period of time will offer a contact number at the end of the work and will emphasise how important it is for you or your child to make contact and ask for further advice if there are any difficulties. Many parents can benefit from the opportunity to speak to someone who can offer advice and listen when things are difficult. You can ask a professional about any other specific local services that might offer support to you on general parenting issues. You may also wish to use a confidential helpline service, such as those provided by NSPCC (0808 800 5000) or the Samaritans (08457 90 90 90) or Parentline (0808 800 2222).

   Although it is natural to want to put your child's sexually abusive behaviour behind you, it is important to recognise that there are likely to be some situations in the future that will test both your child's and your own progress. Key points in your child's future development will need particular attention. These may include:

- Entering into puberty (for children and young people who have not yet started to develop in this way).
- Your child establishing a relationship with a girlfriend or boyfriend.
- Periods of stress and pressure; e.g. exam time.
- The death of relatives or friends; e.g. grandparents.
- Your child leaving home and living independently.
- Your child becoming a parent himself.

   It is important to pay particular attention to issues of support and risk at these times. It may be that the situation itself does not create a direct risk, but it might place your child in a position of stress where his personal resources to maintain the changes he has made are lower.

Final thoughts

Teenage years are generally full of unpredictability and uncertainty, as young people make the transition from child to young adult. Your child's sexually abusive behaviour has interrupted this process. In addition, your child has faced the challenge of making the transition from abusive to healthy sexuality. With your help, support, dedication and love, your child should be better placed to make these changes. The end of the book is unlikely to be the end of your journey, but I hope that you may have been able to find some optimism in the book and that you can hold onto this when faced with the challenges that still lie ahead.

Writing this book has also made me think back to many of the journeys made by the young people and families I have been involved with. Looking back, I feel a sense of curiosity about the futures of many of these young people and their families. To have been a part of their struggles in facing up to their abuse has been a great privilege for me and I have learnt many lessons about myself on the way. I hope that I have done justice to their stories and, importantly, that I have respected their victims, in writing this book.

If the book has helped you in any way face up to your future with hope, the efforts and struggles I have had in writing it will have been more than worthwhile. I wish you all the best.

Exercise 26: Learning to live as a family again

Purpose. This exercise is designed to help you consider some of the key questions relating to rehabilitation of your child.

1. Use the following tables to assess how far the following 'best possible' conditions for rehabilitation have been met in your family. Put a tick in the columns you feel apply in your case.

1.1 Young person who has sexually abused has been able to:	Not at all	Partly	Mostly	Completely
• Take full responsibility for the sexual abuse				
• Understand the impact of his behaviour on the victim and has been able to express concern for the victim				
• Express genuine concern and is sorry for the abuse and, where appropriate, has apologised				
• Understand why he sexually abused				
• Realise what ongoing risk situations are and can talk about these to you as parents and get help outside the family if necessary				

1.2 You as parents have been able to:	Not at all	Partly	Mostly	Completely
• Put the victim's need for protection first				
• Talk to your child and express your feelings about the abuse				

• Discuss the impact of the abuse upon yourselves with your partner				
• See your child as responsible and do not blame the victim				
• Accept the differing needs of the victim, and the young person who has abused, and yet feel that there is a place for meeting both in your family				
• Make changes in your parenting style and skills, and your family, that were needed				
• See the importance of continuing to monitor risk situations				

1.3 Victim of the abuse (if a sibling):	Not at all	Partly	Mostly	Completely
• Has been able to acknowledge and discuss the sexual abuse				
• Knows that the abuse was not her fault and does not blame herself for the young person getting into trouble				
• Wants the young person who has abused to be united with the whole family				
• Is confident that she could report any further abuse and knows who she could talk to				
• Feels safe and protected in the home if the brother or sister who abused is there				

1.4 The whole family agrees that:	Not at all	Partly	Mostly	Completely
• The young person should come home				
• Everyone needing or wanting help has had it offered. All the work needed has been done: or is sufficiently underway to allow confidence that it will be successfully completed.				
• The possible risk situations have been shared and there is a protection plan in place, which everybody agrees to stick to and which involves people outside of the family.				
• Boundaries are strong in the family and people are open with each other.				
• Any relationship difficulties have been talked about and progress made.				
• Any physical issues in the home requiring attention have been addressed, e.g. location of bedrooms, etc.				

2. Review your responses above. Pay particular attention to any issues which you marked as 'not at all' or 'only partly' done. What does this tell you about what else needs to happen to make it possible or safe for your child to return home? Think about this in relation to the following categories:

2.1 What needs to change to make it safer for the victim:

2.2 What else we need to do as parents:

2.3 What else the young person who has abused needs to do:

2.4 What else needs to change about the family as a whole:

Exercise 27: Holding onto change and moving on

Purpose. This exercise is designed to help you to review the important changes that you, the child who abused and your whole family have been able to make since the abuse first came to light.

1. Think back and weigh up what has changed since the time that the abuse was discovered. List the five most important changes for the various people listed.

	You	Your child	Your family	The victim (if also in your family)
1.1				
1.2				
1.3				
1.4				
1.5				

2. Overall, what has improved the most and what is still difficult?

....

....

3. What challenges do you see that lie ahead?

....

....

4. What assurances and commitments can you make for yourself and others about the future?

....

....

Exercise 28: Setting goals for the future

Purpose. This exercise is designed to help you think about the goals, hopes and aspirations you have for the future. These should be realistic and achievable.

1. Consider all the goals, hopes and aspirations you have for the future. You may wish to do this alone or with your partner. Write down your ideas on a separate piece of paper. Do not worry about the order of these: let your ideas flow as much as possible.

2. Now review your list of goals. Separate them into goals for now, for the short-term and the longer-term. Use the following grid to think about what needs to happen to make it more likely that you will reach these goals. Use the first column to be as specific as possible about the goal and who it refers to. Use the final column to think about anything that could get in the way of the goal being achieved and to identify how to overcome these barriers.

	What the goal is:	What needs to happen now to achieve this goal:	What might block the goal and how to over-come the barrier:
Immediate goals			
Between now and five years time			
Over five years			

References

Abel, G., Rouleau, J., and Cunningham-Rathner, J. (1986). Sexually Aggressive Behaviour. In Curran, W., McGarry, A., and Shah, S. (Eds.). *Psychiatry and Psychology: Perspectives and Standards for Interdisciplinary Practice*. Philadelphia, Pennsylvania: SFA Davis Publishing.

Barber, J., and Delfabbro, P. (2000). Predictors of Adolescent Adjustment: Parent–Peer Relationships and Parent–Child Conflict. *Child and Adolescent Social Work Journal*, 17(4): pp. 275–288.

Baumrind, D. (1991). Parenting Styles and Adolescent Development. In Brooks-Gunn, J., Lerner, R., and Petersen, A. (Eds.). *The Encyclopedia of Adolescence*. New York: Garland.

Beckett, R., and Brown, S. (in progress). Multi-site Research on Young People who Sexually Abuse. In Calder, M.C. (2001). *Juveniles and Children who Sexually Abuse: Frameworks for Assessment* (2nd edn.). Lyme Regis: Russell House Publishing.

Calder, M.C. (2001). *Juveniles and Children who Sexually Abuse: Frameworks for Assessment* (2nd edn.). Lyme Regis: Russell House Publishing.

Erooga, M., and Masson, H. (Eds.) (1999). *Children and Young People who Sexually Abuse Others: Challenges and Responses*. London: Routledge.

Finkelhor, D. (1984). *Child Sexual Abuse: New Theory and Research*. New York: Free Press.

Hackett, S., Print, B., and Dey, C (1998). Brother Nature? Therapeutic Intervention with Young Men who Sexually Abuse their Siblings. In Bannister, A. (Ed.). *From Hearing to Healing. Working with the Aftermath of Child Sexual Abuse* (2nd edn.). London: Wiley.

Hanks, H. (2001). Children and Young People's Sexual and 'Normal' Psychosexual Development, Knowledge and Behaviour. In Calder, M.C. *Juveniles and Children who Sexually Abuse: Frameworks for Assessment*, pp. 77–85. Lyme Regis: Russell House Publishing.

Herdt, G., and McClintock, M. (2000). The Magical Age of Ten. *Archives of Sexual Behavior*, 29(6): pp. 587–606.

Johnson, C. (1994). *Children's Natural and Healthy Sexual Behaviours and Characteristics of Children's Problematic Sexual Behaviours*. Self-published.

Johnson, T.C. (1988). Child Perpetrators: Children who Molest Other Children: Preliminary Findings. *Child Abuse and Neglect*, 12: pp. 219–229.

Maccoby, D. (2000). Parenting and Its Effects on Children: On Reading and Misreading Behaviour Genetics. *Annual Review of Psychology*, 51: pp. 1–58.

Messer, D., and Jones, F. (Eds.) (1999). *Psychology and Social Care*. London: Jessica Kingsley.

Mitchell, K., and Wellings, K. (1998). First Sexual Intercourse: Anticipation and Communication. Interviews With Young People in England. *Journal of Adolescence*, 21: pp. 717–726.

Monck, E., and New, M. (1996). *Report of a Study of Sexually Abused Children and Adolescents and Young Perpetrators of Sexual Abuse who were Treated in Voluntary Agency Community Facilities*. London: HMSO.

NSPCC (2000). *Child Maltreatment in the United Kingdom*. London: NSPCC.

O'Callaghan, D., and Print B. (1994). Adolescent Sexual Abusers. In Morrison, T., Erooga, M., and Beckett, R. (Eds.). *Sexual Offending Against Children: Assessment and Treatment of Male Abusers*. London: Routledge.

Office for National Statistics (2000). *General Household Survey*. Office for National Statistics.

Pithers, W., Gray, A., Cunningham, C., and Lane, S. (1993). *From Trauma to Understanding: A Guide for Parents of Children with Sexual Behavior Problems*. Brandon, Vt: Safer Society Press.

Richardson, G., Graham, F., and Bhate, S. (1995). A British Sample of Sexually Abusive Adolescents: Abuser and Abuse Characteristics. *Criminal Behaviour and Mental Health*, 5: pp. 187–208.

Ryan, G., and Lane, S. (Eds.) (1991). *Juvenile Sex Offenders: Causes, Consequences and Corrections*. Lexington: Lexington books.

Ryan, G., Miyoshi, T.J., Metzner, J.L., Krugman, R.D., and Fryer, R.G. (1996). Trends in a National Sample of Sexually Abusive Youths. *Journal of the American Academy of Child and Adolescent Psychiatry*, 33: pp. 17–25.

Strand, P. (2000). Responsive Parenting and Child Socialization: Integrating Two Contexts of Family Life. *Journal of Child and Family Studies*, 9(3): pp. 269–281.

Trotter, J. (1998). *No-one's Listening: Mothers, Fathers and Child Sexual Abuse*. London: Whiting and Birch.

Worling, J., and Curwen, T. (2000). Adolescent Sexual Offender Recidivism: Success of Specialised Treatment and Implications for Risk Prediction. *Child Abuse and Neglect*, 24(7): pp. 965–982.

Help and Support

Selected book resources

There are few books or booklets written for parents whose children have displayed abusive or problematic sexual behaviours. Most of those available are North American. These are some of the best known:

- Johnson, T.C. (1999). *Understanding your Child's Sexual Behavior. What's Natural and Healthy.* New Harbinger Publications. ISBN 1-57224-141-1.

    This American book is one of the few about sexual behaviour problems written for parents. It focuses particularly on younger children, i.e. up to puberty, in contrast to *Facing the Future.*

- Kahn, T. (1997). *Pathways Guide for Parents of Youth Beginning Treatment* (2nd edn.). Brandon: The Safer Society Press.

    A 48-page American book written for parents of young people who have abused, particularly to accompany the Pathways Guided Workbook for Youth Beginning Treatment.

- Pithers, W., Gray, A., Cunningham, C., and Lane, S. (1993). *From Trauma to Understanding: A Guide for Parents of Children with Sexual Behavior Problems.* Brandon: The Safer Society Press.

    This 32-page American booklet is written for parents whose children have abused.

There are more resources for adult survivors of childhood sexual abuse. Two of the best-known are:

- Bass, E., and Davis, L. (1988). *The Courage to Heal: A Guide for Women Survivors of Child Sexual Abuse.* New York: Harper and Row.

- Lew, M. (1993). *Victims no Longer. A Guide for Men Recovering from Sexual Abuse.* London: Cedar.

    An American book which was written for male survivors.

For a comprehensive source of professional information and materials see:

- Calder, M.C. (2001). *Juveniles and Children who Sexually Abuse: Frameworks for Assessment* (2nd edn). Lyme Regis: Russell House Publishing.

Organisations that can offer support and help

There are a range of organisations that can offer help and support in relation to sexual abuse. Some of these will be specific to your local area and you will be able to find information about these from your local social services department or library. Some of these larger national organisations offer helplines:

- **NPSCC** has a freephone helpline (0808 800 5000) where you can report concerns about child abuse and seek guidance and support.

- **Parentline** is a national UK charity which offers a free confidential service for anyone, parent, step-parent, grandparent or foster carer, looking after a child. The freephone helpline number is 0808 800 2222. The helpline is staffed by trained volunteers who are parents themselves. The Parentline organisation also offers a series of training courses for parents in the UK, one of which is called *Parenting Teenagers*.

- **Samaritans** is a charity based in the UK and Republic of Ireland which provides confidential emotional support to anyone who is suicidal or experiencing depression. Samaritans operates a helpline on 08457 90 90 90 (local call costs).

- **Childline** is the UK's national helpline for children and young people in trouble or danger. The Childline freephone number is 0800 1111.

- **Women's Aid** is a national charity in England for women and children experiencing physical, sexual or emotional abuse in their homes. Women's Aid operate a national helpline on 08457 023 468 (local call costs) for women experiencing domestic abuse or violence and others seeking help on their behalf.

Internet resources

If you have access to the Internet there are a range of websites that offer parents help and support in respect of parenting issues. The following sites may contain helpful information:

http://www.parentline.co.uk Website for the UK charity Parentline which offers lots of useful information for parents.

http://www.womensaid.org.uk An internet site for Women's Aid organisation which advises on domestic violence. This site has lots of important advice and contact information.

http://www.samaritans.org.uk Samaritans UK website.

http://www.nspcc.org.uk NSPCC UK website.

http://mencap.org.uk UK organisation working with people with a learning disability.

http://childdevelopmentinfo.com Comprehensive USA site of the Child Development Institute, with lots of advice for parents on issues concerning children and parenting.

Index